Listen, Compose, Perform

A Complete course leading to GCSE

Geoffrey Winters

Contents

D1407184

Longman

Acknowledgements

We are grateful to the following for permission to reproduce copyright material:

Boosey & Hawkes Music Publishers Ltd for extracts from the Concerto for Orchestra by Bartók © Copyright 1946 by Hawkes & Son (London) Ltd. 'Hungarian Folk Song' by Bartók from *For Children Book 2* © Copyright 1946 by Boosey & Co Inc. 'The Virgin Mary had a Baby Boy' from *The Edric Connor Collection* © Copyright 1945 by Boosey & Co Ltd; J & W Chester/Edition Wilhelm Hansen London Ltd for an extract from *Histoire du soldat* by Stravinsky; International Music Publishers for an extract from 'Somewhere' from *West Side Story* by Leonard Bernstein & Stephen Sondheim © 1957, 1959 by Bernstein & Sondheim.

The copyright works Bartók Concerto for Orchestra, 'The Virgin Mary had a Baby Boy' from *The Edric Connor Collection* and Bartók 'Hungarian Folk Song' from *For Children Book 2* are specifically excluded from any blanket photocopying arrangements.

A Teacher's Book and a cassette accompany this book
By the same author
Music Theory in Practice Books 1, 2, 3, and 4
Pick and Mix Music 1 (Recorder Book, Guitar Book, Parts Book, Teacher's Book)
Pick and Mix Christmas (Recorder Book, Teacher's Book)
Sounds and Music Books 1, 2, and 3

LONGMAN GROUP UK LIMITED
Longman House
Burnt Mill, Harlow, Essex CM20 2JE, England
and Associated Companies throughout the World

First published 1986
Second impression 1987
ISBN 0 582 33154 4
Set in 11/13pt Palatino (Linotron)

Printed in Great Britain
by Hazell Watson & Viney Limited, Aylesbury

Composing section

Contents

Introduction

Painters, sculptors and architects arrange and organise their ideas in space. We look at a painting or building from one spot or *we* move to another place to get a different or better view.

Writers and composers organise and arrange their ideas in time. We read a book, watch a play or listen to a piece of music and follow it as it moves past us. We cannot know just how the story may unfold although we may start to guess.

Listening to music is like trying to unroll a length of intricately patterned wallpaper which, as you unroll one end, rolls up at the other, so that at any one time only a small area is visible. You do not know what is coming (until you start to remember the pattern), and you have to recall in your mind what has just gone.

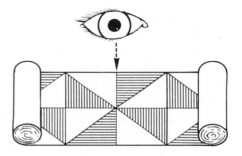

The designs on wallpaper are usually spaced with great care both for their visual impact and so that they will fit. In music the spacing of sounds is equally important.

Visual artists, writers and composers try to place their ideas so that they will grasp the attention of the viewer or listener. Sometimes they try to shock, sometimes they aim to satisfy. They repeat ideas for balance and so that those ideas can be remembered. They move their ideas about to give variety and shape. Unless they are trying to create chaos, they do not throw too many ideas at us at once. They develop one or two ideas for maximum effect so that their work gains a sense of unity.

Composition is to do with organising sounds so that they are good to play and to hear. Quite simple ideas can be developed so that they take us with them as we play or listen. Sometimes the sounds are just pleasant and entertaining, sometimes the music moves us deeply.

Some music is in *free time*. This kind of music is like talking; the sounds are grouped together to make sense, and there are pauses and silences which keep us in suspense as we listen for the next sounds. Music in free time is often gripping and expressive. But mo music has a regular beat and is in *strict time*. This does not mean that it sounds like a machine, but that it has a vital pulse, which can be quick, slow or any pace between. Even the silences are rhythmic and add life to the music, which as it carries us along makes us want to join in with our head, hands and feet.

Now, all you need to start to compose yourself is one small idea!

1 'That's a good idea'

I expect you have often said, 'I've got a good idea, let's—'.

Musical composition, like painting, writing, designing and researching, starts with an idea. One idea leads to another and then to another and so on. Sometimes the first idea is left behind, because some of the other ideas which it has given rise to are much better and more suitable for the purpose in hand. It would be no good having a wonderful idea for a wedding march if you were really trying to compose a lament because the local football team had just missed the cup!

Have you a good idea? Never mind if you haven't. You can borrow one for the time being and almost certainly it will breed a new idea of your own and then you can give the first one back.

What is a musical idea? Well, it could be almost anything. Some ideas come from your mood or feelings: either now, in the past, or even what you think you will feel like if such and such happens in the future. Other ideas come because you know something about the people who will play or hear your music. Others come because you can imagine what will sound best on the instruments available. Many ideas come from the challenge of trying something different, or from searching for a solution to a musical problem. Often the occasion for which the music is to be written will spark off an idea. Is the music for dancing? for relaxing? for welcoming important visitors? for a background to a scene in a play or your holiday snap shots? These are some of the things which will set your mind searching for an idea. There are hundreds more like these, but luckily, somewhere deep down inside you are thousands, if only you can bring them to the surface. On one day you will find it hard to come up with a single good idea, but the next day you may find they come so fast that you will have to work really hard to capture them all on paper or tape before they get away.

Some ideas are over in a flash like these:

a light-hearted word like 'frizzle'

a hollow moaning owl sound, 'toowhit'

a very, very short loud sound

a length of foil torn from its box

a flam on a snare drum

a slide on a xylophone or trombone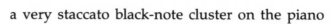

a very staccato black-note cluster on the piano

a couple of slurred notes on a recorder

a single chord for four voices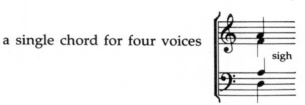

a fierce stroke across a guitar with
the finger nails, immediately damped

a graphic to turn into any appropriate sound.

Try some out and then see if you can think of some more.

Some ideas take a few moments like these:

two or three words like 'frizzle, frazzle, fruzzle'

an owl sound and answer 'toowhit-toowhoo'

a very, very short loud sound followed by the quietest sound yo
can hear held for five seconds

a long rattle on a sheet of foil starting slowly and getting quicker

a shake on a tambourine cut off
by a flam on a snare drum

a slide up and down on a xylophone or trombone
followed by three very short repeated notes

a loud black-note cluster, crushed on to a soft
white-note cluster on the piano

a short dancing melodic motive on a recorder

a nail–pad–nail guitar stroke left to vibrate

a two-chord progression for four voices

another graphic.

Try these out and then find out some more.

Some ideas are for the overall shape of a piece and may take
several minutes or longer to be realised when they are eventually
performed. Here is a selection of larger-scale ideas; you may have
some of your own.

a piece for spoken chorus using families of nonsense words
a piece for five singers inspired by bird sounds
a piece which starts with a bang, drops almost to silence, and then
   very, very slowly grows louder again until a final bang is again
   followed by silence
a piece which contrasts very spiky, dry sounds (perhaps a xylophone
   with wooden beaters) with long bell-like clusters of sounds
   (perhaps a glockenspiel with two players or a piano with the
   sustaining pedal down)
a piece for a very high instrument and a very low one (perhaps a
   piccolo and a bassoon, or a tin whistle and an oil can)
a piece where three similar instruments swap ideas in a conversation.

Notice that in these ideas, not only is the instrument, voice or
material named, but also the way it is to be played, e.g. loud, quick,

spiky, hollow and so on. In some music the interplay of rhythm, melody and harmony is so expressive that the particular speed or loudness may not matter too much. But in other music the effect of colour or timbre (choice of instrument or voice), dynamic (loud or soft), tempo (quick or slow) and articulation (smooth or detached) is almost as important in expressing the mood as the rhythm and notes.

Your idea may strike you with a clear picture of the way it is to be played. If it does not, try to imagine the way it might sound best. Mark your music so that you and others can see the way to play it.

Here are some possible ways which you might consider.

Choice of voice:

adult, child or in between;
high (soprano, treble; tenor), low (alto, contralto; bass) or middle range (mezzo-soprano; baritone);
light-coloured, dark, sweet, harsh or nasal (and so on);
single voice, small group, choir

Choice of instrument:

classroom or orchestral according to ability of players;
string, woodwind, brass, percussion, keyboard, guitar;
played in normal way or perhaps with mute or plucked

Tempo:

slow, fast, moderate or any other speed (but remember to be practical, as some players may not be able to play just the speed you would like);
show speed with Italian terms, in your own language or with metronome marks (remember changes in speed during a piece, like slowing down)

Dynamics:

very soft to very loud;
show with initial of Italian words (f means *forte* or loud), or in your own language (although this is often clumsy);
show changes of loudness with words or with hairpins (◁—)

Articulation:

smooth, joined sound (legato) – leave unmarked or show with slurs;
broken, detached, spiky sound (staccato) – show with dots, above or below the notes, or if it is to carry on for a long time mark staccato

Remember to keep in mind these different ways of presenting ideas when you write your music.

2 Making an idea grow

Look at the ways an idea can grow.

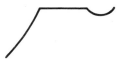

It can be repeated straightaway

or divided into parts and then repeated

or turned round, or upside down

or repeated with a slight variation.

Sometimes the idea will be repeated higher or lower in sequence.

or the intervals stretched

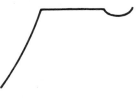

or shrunk

or changed in some other way.

The idea might be extended

or it might grow organically as one part gives rise to the next like a plant.

Now look at the way an idea might grow in musical notation.

original idea

original idea repeated

divided into parts and repeated

turned round and upside down

repeated with a slight variation

in sequence higher and lower

interval stretched

interval shrunk

idea changed in other ways

idea extended

idea grown organically as one part gives rise to another like a plant

Look now in more detail at the way ideas grow in music.

y repetition The easiest way to make an idea grow is to repeat it over and over again like this:

beeperty bop | beeperty bop | beeperty bop | and so on

or this:

 and so on

or this:

and so on.

Just repeating an idea can become monotonous, although the repeated idea can be used as a backing to something else. It is also difficult to know when to stop! A fade-out is often the best way to end here.

Variety can be introduced by presenting ideas in the following ways:

a.   pass the idea round a group of people so that each speaks it with a different tone or level of voice

b.   pass a rhythmic idea across a number of instruments so that eac gives its own colour

c.   pass an idea to a number of positions in the room so that the sound comes from different directions.

Try out some of these ways with the three examples given above.

Idea bank	
a pair of words like *pumpkin* and *pomegranate*	a swirl of rice or sand in a container followed by a number of taps
a rhythmic figure	a vocal 'ah' modified with hand pats in front of the mouth
a melodic motive	a graphic to turn into sound

Now make up your own ideas or borrow from the idea bank and make them grow by straight repetition. Improvise, but if it is with other people, first agree the method of treatment and plan for ending.

By dividing and turning

As you will have found out, repeating an idea over and over again has its problems. When do you stop? When do you breathe? Music, like all living things, must breathe.

When an idea lasts longer than a flash, it can usually be divided into parts. Then the parts can be repeated two or three times like this:

beeperty bop | beeperty bop | beeperty beeperty | beeperty bop |

or this:

beeperty bop | beeperty bop | beeperty bop | bop bop bop |

or this:

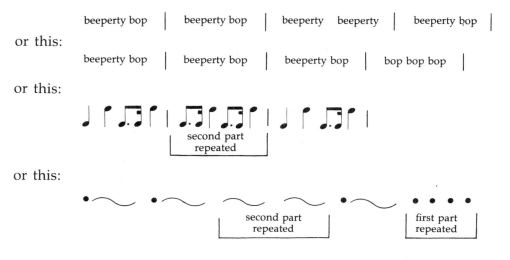

or this:

or turned round like this:

These small changes give shape and direction as well as variety. Nothing new is added; the divisions are still 'one of the family'. The music seems to breathe and to fall into phrases. The phrases could now be repeated several times.

+ 4

Phrases may be of any length. If the music is in strict time, phrases of two and of four bars are common.

Schubert: *Ecossaise* D 529 no. 8

A four-bar phrase is often balanced with another of four bars, especially in dance music, where a number of steps in one direction are answered with a similar number back.

5 + 2 + 2 + 3

However, phrases of other lengths like three and five bars occur, an
a five-bar phrase, for example, may quite happily be answered with
repeated two-bar phrase followed by one of three bars.

Hungarian folksong

4+4+2+2+4

A common phrase structure is paralleled in verse:

There was an – – – – – – – – – – – o,
Who – – – – – – – – – – – – – – o,
He – – – – – – – – o,
And – – – – – – – o,
That – – – – – – – – – – – – – o.

I am sure you know plenty of limericks with which to fill in the bla

In free time there is no steady pulse. Bar-lines do not occur at
regular intervals, but the music must still breathe and be shaped int
phrases. The exact length of time of the phrases is unimportant.
Listeners do not count in seconds. As soon as they have heard one
phrase they listen for the next. Deep down they may have a feeling
for the way a phrase will go and the time it will last. If, when they
hear it, it resembles what they felt, it will satisfy them. If it does no
they will sit up and listen even harder for the next phrase.
Composing in free time needs great care, for you must organise the
sounds to make sense.

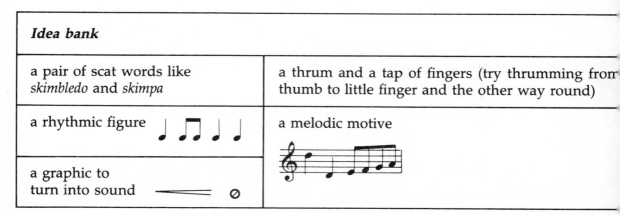

Idea bank	
a pair of scat words like *skimbledo* and *skimpa*	a thrum and a tap of fingers (try thrumming from thumb to little finger and the other way round)
a rhythmic figure	a melodic motive
a graphic to turn into sound	

Find your own ideas or borrow from the idea bank.
Form them into phrases by repeating them whole or in parts.
Choose your instruments and voices carefully.
Fix a tempo.
Remember the effect of dynamics and articulation on your music.

Improvise or write down your ideas. If you are writing in strict time use time signatures and bar-lines. If you are writing in free time, either set out your notes and symbols across the page in a way which will freely show their spacing in time, or if that spacing is to be more accurate, set them out over a time scale like this:

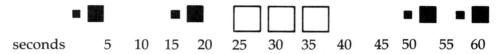

seconds   5   10 15 20 25 30 35 40 45 50 55 60

y raising or owering

When we speak we change the pitch of our voice for variety. Think of the number of ways we can say 'oh': in shock, surprise, wonder or disappointment. Our voice usually goes up when we are excited and falls when we are down in the dumps. In the same way, musical ideas can be sung or played at different pitches like this:

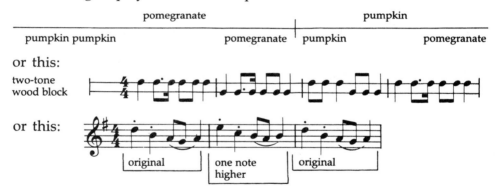

or this:

or this:

When a melodic idea or motive follows on at a different pitch it is called a sequence. Sequences need not move just one note up or down.

Here the original is first turned round and then it and the turned-round version are played in a sequence a 4th lower.

Sequences need not always be exact.

Where has the sequence been changed here? How is it different?

Useful as they are, sequences should not be over-used. Avoid this by making slight changes to their melodic and rhythmic patterns.

Look at the fourth bar. How has the sequence been altered? Notice the way the last bar has been changed to bring the tune to an end. Sequences are like brothers and sisters. They have a strong family likeness so that the unity of the music is maintained.

Idea bank

a name like *lesser spotted woodpecker* to be said at different pitch levels	thrums and taps of fingers on different surfaces, e.g. paper, desk top, book etc
a rhythmic figure to be played on three drums at different pitches	a melodic motive
a graphic to turn into sound to be played or sung at different pitches	

Make up your own ideas or borrow from the idea bank. Repeat, divide and turn them into phrases and longer pieces with some sequences. Make slight changes to the sequences to help the shape of the phrase and add variety. Sequences may be at any interval above or below the original although those that move up or down a step are most common.

Experiment with strict and free time.

Improvise or write out your piece remembering to indicate voice or instrument, tempo, dynamics and articulation.

If your music is non-melodic or experimental, draw a line across the page to provide a reference for pitch level.

The pitch may be widely spaced or alternatively very close, even in micro-intervals. Experiment with both ways.

By stretching and shrinking and changing shape in other ways

Sequences are sometimes changed slightly to improve a phrase or avoid the obvious. The shape of any idea can be changed in a similar manner, but should keep its family likeness in some way.

This:

can become this:

or this:

or this:

or even this:

They all keep the same rhythm, all except the last have a repeated note between the first and second beats, and like the original they mostly move by step. They are like cousins!

Even the last repeats the note E, but an octave higher; it is this jump at the beginning which gives character to this version. After the upward leap, the melody turns inwards and again moves by step. Patterns like this can be stretched or shrunk to embrace other intervals.

Their adaptability is a great help in moving a tune towards its climax. Changed ideas like these can be strung together in phrases and sentences in hundreds of ways. Here are just two examples. Can you see the way they are put together?

Neither tune comes to an end. If they are to sound finished, then another change must be made at the end,

The weakness of these two tunes is that each two-bar section has exactly the same rhythm. When this goes on so long it becomes boring. A small change to the rhythm of one or two bars makes all the difference and will not spoil the family likeness if it keeps close

to the patterns already there, like this:

where extra quavers are added to smooth out the first bar, or this:

where the repeated note idea comes again in the second bar, or this:

where two leaping bars lead towards a climax, or this:

where the pairs of quavers in the first bar occur on other beats to give a push onwards, or this:

where a change of time pushes on the music unexpectedly.

A change of time can be very effective, but be careful, as it can sound just like a mistake.

Idea bank

some words like *astrological signs* to say with different tunes and textures	a rhythmic figure to distribute among several instruments
a melodic motive to change shape **a.** **b.** **c.**	a graphic to turn into sound and shrink and stretch

Select an idea from the idea bank or think up one of your own. Change its shape in a number of ways but make sure it is still 'one of the family'. Join up a number of versions into longer tunes and sentences. Repeat the original if you think this helps your tune to have more unity. Make small changes to the rhythm in one or two bars to break the regularity.

Although a change of shape is most easily applied to a melodic idea, other ideas can be treated in a similar or parallel way.

Word ideas

Speak the words with different 'tunes' or inflections

e.g.

or change the texture of the words by speaking them solo, in small or large groups, or in male, female or mixed groups.

Rhythmic figures

Distribute rhythmic figures across a number of untuned percussion or other instruments so that each repetition will have a slightly different 'tune' as the instrumentation is changed like this:

As with melodies, make other small changes to break the regularity of the rhythm.

Graphics

Except for the purpose of variety, keep the same spacing in time but shrink and stretch the intervals you select for the symbols.

By extension

Two short phrases are often balanced with a longer phrase. This is often an extension which grows out of the shorter phrase, like this:

fa la lal   fa la lal   fa la la la fa la la la fa la la lal

or this:

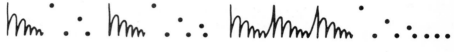

or this:

or this:

Notice the slight change in the second phrase of some examples; for instance, in the melody, the interval is stretched in a near sequence. Notice also the way the ideas are taken forward into the

longer phrase; for instance, the triplet ♩♩♩ from the second phrase of the rhythm occurs at the end of the long phrase.

Finally, notice that the balance is not always mathematically exact; for instance, the longer phrase of the melody lasts five bars, not four as you might expect.

Idea bank

some words to repeat and group into phrases like: *straw* *berry* *jam*	a melodic motive
a rhythmic figure	a mix of humming and open vowels like: m 〜〜〜〜 o n 〜〜〜〜 a
a graphic to turn into sound and extend	

Now find an idea, repeat it exactly or approximately, and then extend it into a longer balancing phrase.

Improvise or write out your pieces; give clear instructions as to the way you wish them to be performed.

By organic growth

An idea can grow organically like a plant. Each new phrase grows out of the previous one as it unfolds.

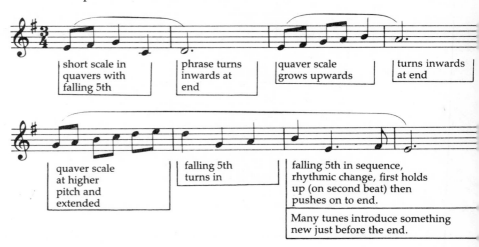

| short scale in quavers with falling 5th | phrase turns inwards at end | quaver scale grows upwards | turns inwards at end |

| quaver scale at higher pitch and extended | falling 5th turns in | falling 5th in sequence, rhythmic change, first holds up (on second beat) then pushes on to end. |

Many tunes introduce something new just before the end.

This tune has a clear, familiar phrase structure. Organic tunes are often quite free and rhapsodic. Their phrase lengths might be quite irregular but they still need to breathe naturally if they are to come alive. Many beautiful tunes grow organically.

Use ideas from the idea bank or make up your own for developing organically. Remember to carry forward elements from one phrase to another allowing them to grow freely.

Experiment with growing words like this:

car

carpet

petrol

trolley-basket

rhythms like this:

and graphics like this:

as well as melodies.

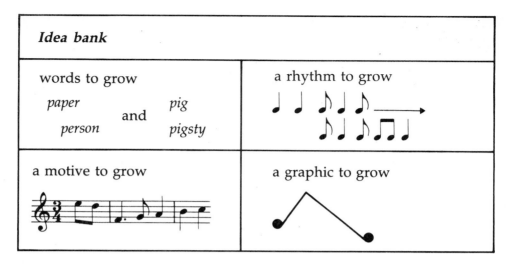

Improvise or write out your pieces and indicate clearly your intentions.

3   Writing a good tune

To most people, a good tune *is* music. They find melodies easiest to remember, whistle and sing and they find melodies quickly pick up their mood. Rhythms, chords and colour are all attractive, but what they really like is a good tune! What about you?

But what is a good tune? It is not always easy to say, but most good tunes have some of the following features.

a.   A mood which is easy to catch; where there are words, the right mood.

b.   A striking idea which is repeated (or nearly repeated) but not done to death.

c.   A nice balance between steps and leaps with perhaps some repeated notes for added character.

d.   A sense of direction and climax.

e.   A clear shape which is easy to follow and ends at the right time in the right place.

Here are some popular melodies which most people would agree were 'good tunes'. Check out the list of features to see whether they 'pass the test'.

Gruber: *Silent Night*

mood	yes	calm, like a lullaby
striking idea	yes	clear rhythmic pattern and melodic shape; easily spotted as it is carried forward in different forms
balance	yes	mostly small leaps between chord notes with some steps and repeated notes
direction and climax	yes	despite repeated bars and phrases, tune move onwards all the time to the climax in the ninth bar
clear shape	yes	mostly in two-bar phrases with a strong pull homewards at the end

Slowly

Bernstein: *West Side Story*, 'Somewher

mood	yes	yearning but confident
striking idea	yes	rising interval in first bar, falling figure in second bar and quaver–dotted crotchet rhythm in middle section all distinct and memorable
balance	yes	leaps set off against smoother movement by step in triplet crotchets
direction and climax	yes	tune moves to climax in middle and then at end; tonic is avoided at the end of each section so that music flows on towards the final long E flat
clear shape	yes	four eight-bar phrases plus five-bar coda at the end

Elgar: *Pomp and Circumstance*, March no. 1, Trio

mood	yes	broad and majestic
striking idea	yes	simple and easy to remember; grows by sequence and rhythmic variation (♫ ♩ becomes ♪♩ ♪ in second line)
balance	yes	mostly steps with just a few well-placed leaps of which that in bars 28–9 is most telling
direction and climax	yes	moves on through repeated and sequential phrases to climax just before last line
clear shape	yes	falls into two sections: the first ends on the dominant at the end of line 2, the second balances the first until the climax and then is extended with a sequence of line 2 to bring the music back home to the tonic.

Elgar thought that this tune would 'knock 'em flat'. It certainly became a great favourite with the public, although Elgar did not really like it being associated with the words 'Land of Hope and Glory'.

You may like to find some of your favourite melodies and put them to the test. Make notes about the way they satisfy the features listed. If they have any shortcomings, try to describe them.

Some people seem to write tunes without effort. Schubert was one of these and his melodies just flowed out in a stream. Other people find it harder to write a good melody, although they may be fine at making up lively rhythms, arresting harmonies or exciting blends of instrumental colour. Beethoven often wrestled over and over again with his melodies until he wrenched and bent them into a shape which expressed his feelings and fitted into the piece he was composing. Perhaps you will come somewhere in between.

OPUS

Now try and write a good tune of your own. Think about the examples you have just looked at and at any other tunes which you think are good. Then work along these lines.

Set the mood in your mind or, if the tune is to be sung, take the mood from the words. Search for an idea which suits that mood.

Let the idea grow in some of the ways you have practised.

Keep a balance between leaps, steps and repeated notes.

Shape your tune into phrases as you move onwards. If the tune is in more than one section, the first section should lead towards a note other than the tonic or keynote so that it is open-ended and incomplete. Many tunes arrive at the dominant at the midway mark. The second section leads the music back towards the keynote or other resting place.

Move the music onwards all the time so that it arrives at a climax at just the right place.

Keep in mind for whom you are writing and their ability as a player or singer. It is no good writing a wonderful tune if it is too high to sing or too difficult to play.

4   Chords and clusters

Any group of two or more notes played at the same time is called a chord.

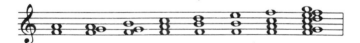

Groups which squash adjacent notes together, like the second and last in the example above, are sometimes called clusters.

The idea of singing different notes at the same time may have happened by accident. Perhaps someone found it hard to keep up with a tune when it went higher and was left behind singing at a lower pitch like this:

There must always have been sopranos and altos, tenors and basses. Certainly the idea of singing in two or more parts must have appealed, for by the 9th century there are written examples of chants in parallel 5ths and 4ths. After this, the taste for richer chords developed gradually over many centuries.

In composition, a chord has almost as many uses as an egg in cooking. You can even scramble it! Here are a few basic ways to use chords. Use your ear and your imagination and look at the rules later.

Drones

Instruments like the bagpipe and hurdy-gurdy play a continuous sound or sounds underneath a melody. This is a drone. It may have been the earliest way that two or more notes were played at the same time.

A drone might be a single sound held continuously

and so on

or it might be a pair of sounds which are often a 5th apart

and so on

or it might be either of these repeated over and over again in a rhythmic pattern.

and so on

A drone may be played on any instrument (or sung), although continuous drones are usually played on a string instrument or other instruments where the player does not have to take a regular breath. Bagpipes solve this by having a bag which can be filled as convenient and then squeezed so that the air comes out and produces a long stream of sound. Alternatively a long note is restarted at the beginning of each or every other phrase.

Music with drones is sometimes slow and expressive, as with a lament. At other times it is really lively like a jig and may have percussion instruments added to it.

OPUS

Choose a melodic and a drone instrument and write a piece for them in sad or lively mood.

hords in ose armony

A simple tune

can be paired with notes a 3rd higher

or a 3rd lower

(when it sounds as if it is in a minor key)
or it can be paired with notes a 6th higher

(which are actually the same notes put up an octave)
or it can be lined up with both 3rds and 6ths in parallel

(which really sounds like harmony)
or with a triad on every note

(which sounds like music from the Far East)

or it can use these same notes an octave lower, underneath the tune in first-inversion chords

(which makes it easier to hear the original tune).

Not all close harmony remains exactly parallel with the tune however. Sometimes it moves up or down while the tune stays still, or the other way round

(which gives the parts a life of their own and makes the music more pleasing to hear).

Close harmony is often mixed with solo or unison passages

(which adds variety to the texture as it moves from one to two or three parts). Harmonising in this simple way has been popular (especially in England) for over six centuries. The music is sometimes written down, but it is quite often improvised, and then unexpected and exciting clashes may occur.

OPUS

Find simple tunes or make up your own. Team them up with other notes in close harmony. Use 3rds and 6ths, or triads and their inversions. Look and listen for places where a little independent movement of the parts will add life. Do not use close harmony all the time. Add variety to the texture by using one, two or three parts at different times.

Chord guide

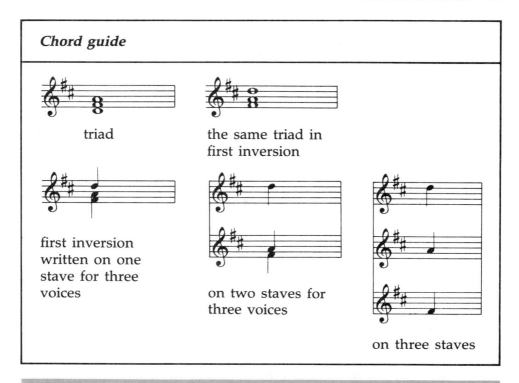

triad

the same triad in first inversion

first inversion written on one stave for three voices

on two staves for three voices

on three staves

hords for .ickening

Sometimes composers need fuller textures than those provided by just three voices or parts.

Voices or strings

So they double the notes an octave higher on other instruments:

Flutes
Clarinets

Voices
or strings

or if a deeper, richer texture is suitable, they double the notes in lower octaves as well or instead (note that in this example the triads are doubled in such a way that they are in root position, instead of in first inversion as before).

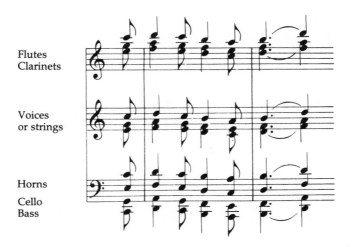

The chords are still triads with only three different notes. All the notes added above and below double the notes of the triads.

Even richer sonorities can be produced by using chords with more than three notes and then doubling some of them, like this:

These are 9th chords, which are built by adding further next-door-but-one notes on to a triad like this:

triad   7th   9th

Chords with 7ths and 9ths were much relished by composers like Debussy, and were used to produce both dreamlike and sonorous sounds. The contrast with lighter textures or silence becomes even more striking with such chords. They look frightening with so many notes, but they are really quite easy to work out. Enjoy their rich flavour in moderation when writing your music.

OPUS

Make up a short progression (two or three chords, in root position or inversion, will be enough) and write them out so that they can be performed in the following ways:

a.   for keyboard or tuned percussion
b.   for voices in three parts
c.   for three wind or string instruments
d.   for three instruments or voices doubled above or below with three other instruments
e.   for three voices or instruments doubled by as many singers and players as you can persuade to take part; extend the range higher and lower.

Do not think that because there are so many performers the music has to be loud. Rich textures are just as effective when soft.

Now convert your progression from triads to 7ths or 9ths (or make up a new one) and perform it as follows.

f.   with four or five players, one to each note of the chord
g.   with the notes of the chords doubled with as many players as possible or desirable.

When you have tried out these short experiments, make up a piece which contrasts rich, thick textures with unison or lighter ones.

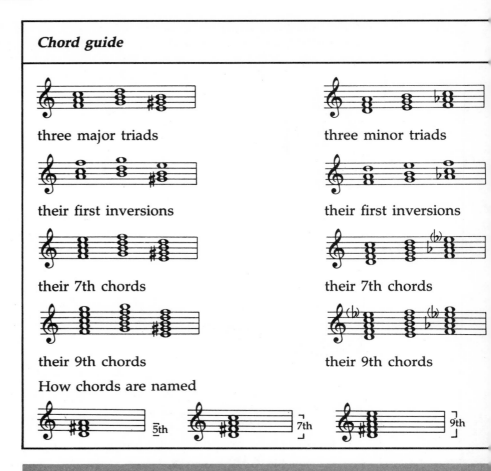

Chord guide

three major triads

their first inversions

their 7th chords

their 9th chords

three minor triads

their first inversions

their 7th chords

their 9th chords

How chords are named

5th   7th   9th

Clusters for thickening

In recent years, some composers have wanted even denser textures to express their thoughts and have used clusters of notes for this purpose. Sometimes these are written out in full as here:

Sometimes only the outside notes are shown, like this:

long sound

short sound

On keyboard instruments, clusters might be played on black or white notes with a flat hand or hands, or even with both forearms over a wide range.

As with thick chords, they do not have to be played loudly. Clusters can be sustained and held on, or be short and staccato. They can be rolled upwards or downwards.

Clusters on other instruments have to be played by groups all playing different notes. Such clusters may be slid up or down in a glissando like this:

starting notes to be played by each instrument

Clusters may be thinned out or thickened as they sound, like this:

Clusters are very effective with groups of voices. Try to hear some of the music of the Hungarian composer Ligeti, who has written quite a number of pieces which make use of clusters.

OPUS

You may have an idea for a cluster piece or feel there is a place in your music where a few clusters would help to express your thoughts. Improvise or write out your ideas using traditional or graphic notation.

Chords and clusters for accents

The shape of a tune or rhythm is often highlighted with chords or clusters like this:

or this:

or the chords and clusters mark the off-beats and jerk the music on in syncopation as here:

Accented chords are usually short or staccato. On string instruments they might be played pizzicato.

OPUS

Find energetic tunes and rhythms or make some up. Accent them with chords and clusters on some of the beats or off-beats so that music is driven on. Experiment to find chords which fit; let your ear be the guide. Like some people, you may find it a help to look at notes used in the tune and 'collect them up' into chords and clusters. Clusters can be formed from all the notes in a bar or a motive; triads (as well as 7th chords) are formed from every other note of a scale; the notes each side of a leap in a melody will probably belong to a chord; and lastly a triad under or over an important note in a motif might be just the sound you are hoping to find. The chord guide on the opposite page may be consulted for more help.

Chord guide

Collect a cluster	Select a step	If it leaps catch it	Try a triad

Use every note in motive, fill in missing steps for complete cluster.	Use every other step of a scale to form a triad.	A jump in a motive points to the notes of a chord. Here A and E outline the triad.	Try a triad under the first or last note.

---

m-cha-cha ords

Thousands of waltzes and other dances in triple time have an um-cha-cha accompaniment like this:

where the triad is split up into a single bass note on the first beat and chords on the second and third beats.

Sometimes the bass note alternates between two notes of the triad to make it more melodic:

and in some bars, a rest is used in place of a chord:

which breaks the regularity of the rhythm, gives the melody some independence, and in addition lightens the texture.

Of the many waltz tunes Johann Strauss wrote, a few were based on just two chords, the chord built on the first degree of the scale, the tonic or I, and the chord on the fifth degree, the dominant or V The dominant chord was mostly used with a 7th for extra colour.

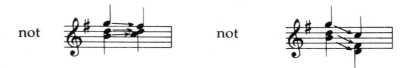

alternating bass notes,
tonic or I

alternating bass notes,
dominant or V

Notice the way the chord moves by step to a close position when it changes. This makes it easy to play and smooth to follow.

not ![music example]   not ![music example]

Strauss's rhythms and melodies are full of variety and vitality and a set off well against such simple harmonic progressions. When he used more chords, he often slipped in the chord of II towards the end of a tune as an approach to V.

OPUS

A Play um-cha-cha accompaniments on a suitable instrument like the piano or guitar. Two players could play the piano, one playing the bass line, the other the chords. On most instruments, the bass will sound best an octave lower than it is shown here. The chord guide will help you find the chords.

Start with a single chord, then add an alternating bass and then change to another chord, every two, four or eight bars. When you are swinging along well, slip in an odd rest on the second or third beat for variety.

B Here is a 16-bar progression from Strauss's waltz *The Gipsy Baron*. Each Roman numeral represents one bar. Improvise um-cha-cha accompaniments as before. First pick an easy key and then try something harder.

$$
\begin{array}{cccc}
I & I & I & I \\
I & I & V_7 & V_7 \\
V_7 & V_7 & V_7 & V_7 \\
V_7 & V_7 & I & I
\end{array}
$$

Notice the way the pattern of chords in the first part is balanced by their reverse in the second part. Progressions like this are the basis for many tunes.

C Similar accompaniments are found in duple and quadruple time. Practise these figures in a number of keys.

Make up progressions with two or more chords in mixed time.

e.g. $\dfrac{2}{4}$ $\dfrac{3}{4}$ $\dfrac{2}{4}$ $\dfrac{4}{4}$ and so on

D Try to find the chord of II and use it as an approach chord to V in your improvisations.

e.g. I I II V₇

E Experiment with mixing up quite different chords like these:

You may find some exciting progression which you can use in your music.

Chord guide

Um-cha-cha accompaniments in:

key of C
(alternative
bass in
brackets)

key of G

key of F

key of A
minor

key of E
minor

Scrambled chords

In many accompaniments, the chords are scrambled into broken chords or arpeggios.

Like eggs, they still have the same content, but now have a different form and effect. They help the music to flow and they lighten the texture.

Some tunes are built round scrambled chords. Bugle calls use just the notes of the tonic chord:

Other tunes may be based on more chords, as here, where chords I and V are broken into separate notes.

However, it is unusual for a tune just to use chord notes.

Here, passing notes, slipped in between chord notes, help to push on the melody.

Many bass riffs are built from scrambled chords:

In this only the single quaver is not in the chord. It is a neighbouring or auxilliary note. Unusually, this riff is in $\frac{5}{4}$ and lasts one bar before it repeats. Most riffs are in quadruple time and last two bars.

OPUS

Here are a number of ways for you to use scrambled chords. Improvise and then write down some of your ideas. Even when you improvise, you may like to make a note of the progressions, so that you can easily repeat them. Either write the actual chord names in bars like this:

F   F   Gm   Gm

or write the chord degrees in Roman numerals.

I   I   II   II

A   Practise scrambling a number of chords into arpeggios and broken chords. Join them up into progressions.

B Make up chord tunes from scrambled chords, adding a few passing or neighbouring notes to keep them moving.

C Make up bass riffs and form them into progressions. Either find yo own chord sequence, or use this traditional three-chord, twelve-bar blues progression.

I   I   I   I
IV   IV   I   I
V₇   V₇   I   I

For a more jazzy style add a neighbouring note at the top of some chords, turning them into 'added sixth chords'.

5   Partnerships

Echo partnerships

The most straightforward partnerships are those which pass an idea back and forth from one person or group to another.

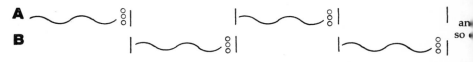

Group or person B echoes an idea before passing it back to A. Variety comes from the contrast of tone or position between the groups. Monotony can be avoided by linking the repetition with changes of dynamic or colour. An end can be made after an agreed number of repetitions, or suddenly at a climax, or gradually with a fade-out.

A more interesting echo partnership is one where person or grou A varies the idea by dividing or turning it while person or group B repeats the original idea as a steady base.

As with straight repetition, changes of dynamic and colour give variety and direction to the piece. Endings can be arranged in similar ways.

Partnerships like this can be developed into a 'follow-the-leader' form where B echoes A as the idea steadily evolves. In improvisation B has to listen carefully to repeat accurately each version.

and
so on

Follow-the-leader partnerships can go on forever, especially when they are improvised, but as before, it is better to agree some form of ending in advance. Alternatively they can end when A follows on and repeats a version in unison, together with B like this:

OPUS

I   Improvise or write down echo partnerships in these three forms. All the ideas which you used earlier in the book may be used in these partnerships. Scat words, natural sounds, rhythms, melodic motives or graphics can be repeated, divided, turned or developed in other ways.

Perform them with voices or instruments. Groups may be equal in size, or unequal (solo or chorus) and be of similar or dissimilar colour or range (high voices answered by low voices, or drums by drums). Indicate or agree tempo and dynamic markings and work out the way your pieces are to end.

Partners in rhythm

When you make up an echo partnership you have to be careful of the way one part follows the other.

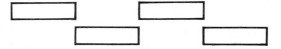

When you make up other forms of partnership you have to be careful of the way the parts fit on top of each other as well.

When you make up a rhythmic partnership be careful that the parts do not get in each other's way. They might share each other's ideas, but they should not be asked, too often, to play them at the same time. Otherwise instead of sounding like a real duet, the music will sound like a solo played by two players.

Here is a duo for a tambourine and a scraper.

Notice

a.   that the scraper plays the same two bars over and over except for the last bar, which is different

b.   that the tambourine enters later and uses the same idea turned round

c.   the rests between the tambourine's phrases

d.   the organic growth of the second phrase.

Most partnerships work best when there is a certain give and take between the partners, as in this duo for a high and low drum.

Notice

a.   the way one part starts off
b.   the way they pass an idea from one to the other
c.   the number of rests which lighten the texture and allow the other part to come through
d.   the way the parts come together at the end and play the same rhythm
e.   the way both parts are enjoyable to play.

OPUS

A   Make up a rhythmic duo with a simple repeated part and a part which is related to it but free. Choose your instruments carefully; or as an alternative use body sounds like clapping and finger clicking.

B   Make up another rhythmic duo in which the partners 'give and take'.

Partners in canon

In a canon both groups or players have the same music, but, as with a round, they do not play it at the same time. One starts off and the other follows at a fixed distance.

Words can be spoken in canon like this:

A   Passengers for flight two-nine-six   Forward to gate fourteen
B   Passengers for flight two-nine-six

In fact in badly adjusted public address systems we sometimes receive the information 'in canon', as we do with sounds in caves and rocky hill areas where the echo overlaps the sound source.

Graphics can be turned into sound and played in canon.

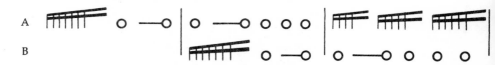

Notice that when B starts, A has different sounds.
Rhythms can be played in canon.

Notice

a.   the way the two parts do not have the same rhythmic figure at the same time except at the end where the triangle repeats a figure to finish with the wood block
b.   the new semiquaver idea in bar 5
c.   that the instruments take it in turns, with plenty of rests
d.   the way the rhythms grow all the time.

Scrambled chords can be put together in canon quite simply if they are based on just *one* chord like this:

Notice
a.   that all the notes except the passing notes in bars 3 and 4 are from a G chord (G, B and D)
b.   that where possible the parts 'steer clear' of each other's notes
c.   that as with rhythmic canons the instruments do not play the same rhythm at the same time
d.   that the parts finish together, with the leader having a couple of notes which are not imitated by the other part.

When making up a canon you must keep an ear on both parts as you extend them. Keep in mind the answering part's phrase as you add the leader's new phrase over it. Build up the music bar by bar. When selecting instruments for canons be sure that both instruments and players are able to manage the same music. It is no good asking a bass drum to play the rapid music which a snare drum can perform.

OPUS

Make up canons using spoken chorus, sound graphics, rhythms and scrambled chords. Maybe you could combine two forms and write a canon say for two rhythmic instruments plus two melodic instruments playing a scrambled chord!
    When you have had more experience at organising sounds you will be able to write canons which combine melodies based on more than

one chord and also write canons where the second part has the sam[
music but at a different pitch, or the same music backwards!

Writing in strict canon is a good discipline, but in your own musi[
you may find it more use to treat canon freely. Such canonic
imitation, as it is known, can be used for a few bars before the mus[
moves on to material which is less strictly organised, such as a
conversation between the instruments, or a contrasting chordal
passage.

Special partnerships

Until this section, each partner in a duo has had the same or a
similar part. But sometimes one partner has something special to gi[
like a rich colour, or an ability to play very fast or to play thick
clusters. Here is a duo for glockenspiel and jingles.

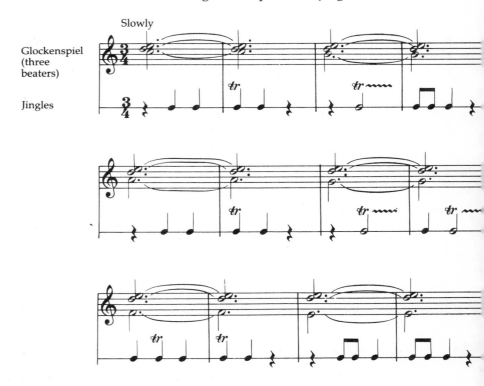

Notice
a. the character of each part: one instrument cannot trill, the othe[
    cannot sustain, but they both give something to the whole
b. the way the glockenspiel plays on the first beat while the jingles re[

c. the simple pattern of the glockenspiel chords, with two beaters
    in the right hand playing the same notes while the left hand
    plays down a scale

d. the way the jingle part grows from the first bar.

Sometimes when people are together one partner will have a bright
idea. A sizzling rhythm on a cymbal may spark off the other partner
like a rocket. This is the way things happen in good jazz extempor-
isation, where the players respond to each other.

Here is the start of a duo for clarinet and cymbal.

Notice

a. the driving cymbal part

b. the way the parts fit together

c. the way the clarinet ideas grow.

Nearly all instruments have some sound which is special to them.
In addition, some are able to make special effects with the help of
mutes or unusual ways of plucking or blowing. Some everyday
objects, like a sheet of hardboard or a saw, have very special sounds.

OPUS

Think of an instrument which you or someone else can play. Write a
duo for it which shows off its special sound against another,
contrasting sound. For instance, the low notes of a flute have a very
special sound; what would they go with?

Accompanying partners

Of all musical partnerships, that between a singer or instrumentalist and an accompanist is the most common. The accompaniment may be of chords or scrambled chords or a combination of both. The tune will usually grow out of the chord progression and will often be built round scrambled chords as well. Unless a special effect is aimed for, melody and harmony will move hand in hand.

Perhaps you have added already a tune to an um-cha-cha accompaniment, or tried a few bars over a bass riff.

Project

Here is part of a waltz for piano. The tune consists mostly of chord notes. The um-cha-cha accompaniment is in the left hand. To keep it simple, the 'cha-cha' chords have been reduced from three to two notes. This gives a lighter texture, which is often an advantage.

Notice

a.   the introduction, which sets the tempo and introduces the basic figure

b.   the non-chord note D at the beginning of each phrase, which is a leaning note or appoggiatura, adding life to the tune

c.   the 2 + 2 + 4 phrase structure, which always starts on the third beat of the bar

d.   that the chords change every two bars in the first line, but then change every bar; this variation adds greater interest.

The bass notes to the remainder of the waltz have been sketched in. Complete the piece by repeating the tune for a few bars before changing it to make it sound finished.

oject

   Here is the start of a song for voice and guitar, in two versions. In the first, the voice uses only chord notes and the guitar scrambles those chords into a simple arpeggio accompaniment. In the second, the melody is smoother and is moved on by non-chord passing and neighbouring notes. The guitar keeps to the same chords but has a more flowing figure.

Notice

a.   the two-bar introduction on the E minor chord which sets the tempo, the key and the mood

b.   the guitar part, which lies under the fingers and uses only chord notes

c.   that the voice also uses only chord notes, e.g. A, C and E over the A minor chord

d.   the two-chord change in bar 5 and the change of bass note in the E minor chord; this gives a smoother, more melodic bass line.

Notice

a. the guitar's semiquaver accompaniment, which gives it more independence

b. at the end of some bars the accompaniment's non-chord notes, which lead towards the next chord

c. the smoother melody, with just a few leaps which outline chord notes

d. the semiquaver figure in the voice part with a slur to show that there are two notes to a word

e. the overall shape of the melody, which moves down over three bars and then finds a mid-way position.

The words to the second part of each version have been set out over the guitar line. Complete the melody of one or both versions keeping it in style with the first part.

roject
Here are the first three bars of a piece for violin and piano. Melody and accompaniment are closely related and move hand in hand.

The ideas for a piece like this might grow in a number of ways. The violin melody could be drawn out of the right-hand piano clusters like this:

or the piano clusters may be 'collected up' from the violin melody.

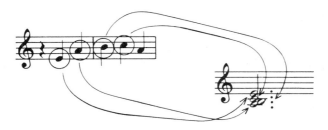

In practice, it is most likely that the composer would use a mixture of methods and switch from one to another as the music developed. A tune would hint at an accompanying chord, or a rhythm might lead to a melody, and so on.

continuation of violin melody

Notice

a. the way the melody and accompaniment are related

b. that the left-hand clusters mostly add colour; their notes are seldom taken into the melody, unlike those in the right hand

c. the shape of the melody, which grows to a climax and then fades away, before being repeated in the continuation

d. the phrase structure: three three-bar phrases followed in the first part by three two-bar phrases and in the second part by four two-bar phrases

e. the ending, which is left in suspense.

Only the violin melody is given for the second part. It is largely a repeat of the first part. Complete the piece by using the original accompaniment where it will fit or by finding other clusters where needed.

OPUS

Now write a song or instrumental duo for you or someone else in your group to sing or play with a piano or guitar. Use chords, scrambled chords or clusters in the accompaniment. Choose a pattern which suits the instrument and, except for small variations, stick to it. Be sure the melody moves hand in hand with the accompaniment.

Tuneful partners

Tunes in partnership are found in a number of forms: a descant over a hymn tune, a second part to a folksong, a counter-melody to an orchestral tune, or a countersubject in a fugue or a two-part piece for instruments or voices. Some of these are accompanied, some are not.

At the simplest, tuneful partners play or sing in parallel close harmony. Both partners have an equal say, but because they follow each other so closely, they are never able to add a little something of their own.

Music in two parts should be like a pair of skaters who flow along together, combining their individual movements into an expressive unity: sometimes in parallel harmony, sometimes touching, sometimes parting, sometimes linking and sometimes spinning away only to join again in their ever onward movement.

Two-part counterpoint, as this type of partnership in music is called, has varied from period to period; sometimes free, at other times strict, it changes rather in the way that etiquette changes.

As with all partnerships, tuneful partners must show some give and take. The two melodies must blend together in a way which makes us sure that they are both on the right notes. This does not mean that they must always join up in the sweeter intervals like 3rds and 6ths, but it does mean that where they do not, the relationship between them must be clear and convincing. In this section it is only possible to give a few pointers to help you write as you wish, but they should help you write in a way that will be enjoyable both to play and to hear.

Points on counterpoint

Chord framework

The two parts should sound as if they belong together. Have in mind a chord framework. Let the notes of each melody grow out of the framework. Then use non-chord notes like passing, leaning and neighbouring notes to give the music life and movement. The chord framework can always be changed if you find the melodies taking off.

Trumpets 1 and 2

chord framework   G |C |C |D minor |

ntrary and lique motion

Each of the two parts should have a life of its own. Let them move in contrary and oblique motion as well as in parallel and similar motion.

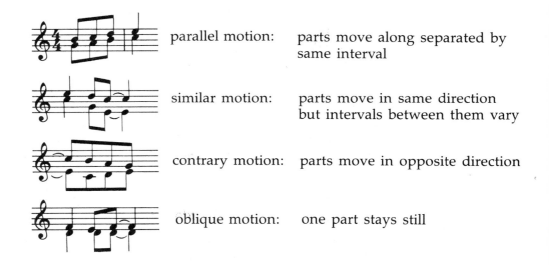

parallel motion: parts move along separated by same interval

similar motion: parts move in same direction but intervals between them vary

contrary motion: parts move in opposite direction

oblique motion: one part stays still

Aim to give both parts enjoyable music to play and sing. As in the examples, mix movement by step with a few well-placed leaps.

1ythmic dependence

Keeping the parts independent in rhythm helps to let them have a life of their own. It adds vitality and allows the interplay between parts to be more clearly heard.

Although with its largely crotchet second part this version is simpler than the earlier example, it is probably as effective and pleasing to hear, if not more so.

Imitation

Musical conversation between the parts adds further variety and individuality. Look out for places where one part can echo the other but do not force it to an exact imitation. Use rests to lighten the texture and set off the entry.

The second-part imitation is an octave and a note lower and is not exact in line or interval. It suggests the idea of the first part.

Interval quality

Intervals have different qualities: 3rds and 6ths sound smooth and comfortable, 4ths and 5ths are open and hollow, 2nds and 7ths unsettled and edgy. All will be affected by their setting in the phrase, where quite dissonant intervals can be lost in the onward movement. The overall style also affects the quality of intervals. In a very dissonant style, a *major* 2nd might even sound a relief. Use the less stable intervals like augmented and diminished 4ths and 5ths, as well as 2nds and 7ths, to keep the music moving. Push on through them to a more restful interval. Look at each example and notice the way the different intervals are used.

Perfect parallels

Like all fashion, the taste for parallel perfect intervals has changed from time to time. In the 10th century, parallel 4th and 5ths were rather favoured. And from late in the 19th century, parallels again came back into fashion in the music of Debussy and others. Between times, the traditional counterpoint of the 16th to 18th centuries did not use parallel perfect intervals, for it wished to keep the parts quite independent. So if you do not wish one part to be a 'copycat' of another, do not let the parts merge into one. To avoid this, use:

NO    NO consecutive unisons   the parts must not play the same notes together, or else two tunes become one

NO  NO consecutive parallel octaves — the parts must not play the same notes an octave apart, for the same reason

NO  NO consecutive parallel perfect 5ths — the parts must not move in parallel perfect 5ths, as this interval is so open and bare that it sounds as if both parts are playing the same tune.

These restrictions are necessary to keep the two parts independent. They do not apply where both parts stay still as here:

Nor do they apply where a part is doubled throughout to thicken the texture, as with so many piano passages in octaves.

Nor do they apply in music which makes a feature of the special quality of perfect 5ths, as in this bell-like example.

The mastery of counterpoint can be a long and serious study. Chords by themselves can become stodgy and static, but when the chords arise from the onward movement of two or more parts, the music springs to life. The performer enjoys weaving a way through the texture and the listener gains pleasure from hearing the interplay of parts, noticing first one and then another come to the surface. The music of many great composers gains strength and vitality from counterpoint.

OPUS

When writing your own music, look out for places where an
independent voice or line will drive it forward. Aim for life and
movement before you worry too much about detail and perfection.
As you and your ear gain experience, you will be able to control
the sounds more fully to the end you have in mind. Before you try
to write a descant, or a second part for a folksong, or a piece for two
voices or instruments of your choice, or any other similar piece, try
and solve the short puzzles which follow. They will help you to start
thinking contrapuntally.

Puzzles

A   Here are four **phrases** which have lost their partners. Look at or play
each phrase on the left-hand side and match it in two-part
counterpoint with one on the right. Write them out, either on one
stave, turning the stems of the notes up or down as necessary, or on
two staves.

B   a.   Add to this phrase an upper part which mostly moves by step in
contrary motion.

b.   Add a lower part for a recorder player who can manage just two notes. Write mostly in minims.

c.   Make up a lower part from

d.   Make up a sequential top part from this pattern

using it, at different pitch levels, wherever there are crotchets in the lower part.

6   Writing for instruments

Just as chefs learn to appreciate the effect of herbs and spices and painters the colours in their palettes, so composers (and arrangers) have to know about the sounds and techniques of the various instruments for which they write. These people learn by using their senses to taste, to look and to listen and they widen their experience by being alert to their own and other people's creations.

It is important to have a feeling for instruments when you compose. This chapter looks at the ways you can help yourself to become more familiar with their sound and techniques.

Finding out about instruments

By listening

The most important way to find out about instruments is to listen to them being played. Listen to your friends practising, listen to their teachers playing, go to local concerts and hear instrumentalists in action and listen to records, radio and television. Even try a few experiments yourself on instruments you do not normally play.

Listen to the quality of the different instrumental families: brass, woodwind, strings, percussion, harp, guitar and keyboards. Listen too for the kind of music they play. Listen to the members of a family and learn to recognise the difference between, for instance, a flute and an oboe. Try to recall their sounds in your head when you are quiet and away from them. Listen to the way an instrument sounds when it is playing low in its register and to the way it sounds in a middle or high range.

Be alert for unusual effects: a mute on a trumpet, flutter-tonguing or a flute or tremolo on an electronic organ.

Once you have started to listen actively, you will be able to ask yourself questions like these:

Which instrument do I feel has the warmest sound?
Which instrument do I feel can make really spiky sounds?
Which instrument would I choose for a brilliant and brittle piece?
Can the trombone play fast enough for the passage I have in mind?
Do I really like the sound of a glissando on the violin?
Which instrument do I think would make a good partner for a bassoon?

Notice that all these questions are addressed to *you*: your responses might be different from other people's and may vary from time to time. I sometimes feel that the viola has the warmest sound, but your choice might be quite different.

Now ask yourself some other questions about the instruments to which you have been listening.

By talking to players

Important as it is to absorb the sound of an instrument, it is also desirable to know something about the way it works and is played. So it is always a good idea to talk to the people who play the instruments.

Ask them about what they find easy and what they find difficult. Ask them to show you what 'lying comfortably under the hands or the fingers' means. Pianists only have five fingers on each hand and often have to pass the thumb under, so the passages they play have to take this into account. String players finger in hand positions. Recorder players do not like rapid passages which involve forked fingering. Woodwind and brass players have to breathe: ask them about the problems involved; ask them also to show you the difference between tongued and slurred notes. Ask a drummer to slow down his paradiddle technique so that you can see and hear the different drum strokes. Do guitarists have any problems? Ask them which is their favourite key and so on.

Find out from players the kind of music they like playing and what they feel suits their instrument. They may like or dislike long held notes, rapid repeated notes, chords, arpeggios, wide jumps and skips, and many, many other devices.

If you are about to write for a certain player or group make sure you know their abilities and ranges. This is very important with inexperienced players, who may find your music strange at first and will not be pleased to have extra problems.

*looking at
sic*

Support your listening and quizzing of players by looking at music written for the various instruments. Which keys are used most? is the instrument used in different registers? does it play outside its middle range very much? does the music leap about or is it more song-like? which patterns and figures occur most often? Does wind music look like string music and are there any markings which are special to an instrument or group? Is there anywhere in the music for wind players to breathe?

studying books

You will not learn what an instrument sounds like by studying a book, but you will be able to check its history, its construction and the way it is played. You will be able to look up its range (both overall and practical) and its use in orchestras. There are many reference books which will help you to increase your knowledge, but do not forget to really listen whenever you have an opportunity.

actical
ide to
rings

wing

The bow is pushed or pulled across the strings to make them vibrate.

A pulled stroke   a stroke which
is called   is pushed
a down-bow,   is called an up-bow.

When the music is unmarked, the player changes the bow direction for each note.

When two or more notes are slurred together they are played in one bow, either up or down.

In compound time, or where there is a succession of long and short notes, it is usual to take two notes in one bow.

This prevents the player 'running out of bow', which easily happens where each long note needs a longer bow stroke. Staccato on a string instrument is usually produced by stopping the bow on the string for a moment between each note, or by bouncing the bo

Plucking

As an alternative to bowing, the strings can be plucked with the finger or, in the case of the cello and bass, with the finger or thum This is called pizzicato and is marked 'pizz.' in the music. The change to pizzicato is easier after an up-bow as the fingers are nea the strings, but some time must be allowed for the switch, especial with inexperienced players.

The return to normal bowing is shown by the word 'arco' (meaning bow).

Hand positions

The left hand stops or shortens the strings to produce higher soun The more the hand can remain in one position the easier the music to play. The violin gives these notes in first position.

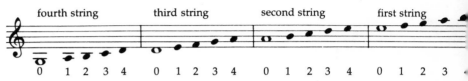

Notice that the notes D, A and E can be played on open strings as stopped notes with the fourth finger. Semitone adjustment is made to give sharps and flats.

By sliding the left hand up to the third position, the player can obtain these notes.

Open strings can be mixed with any position with good effect.

With the exception of the first position, which includes the open strings, each position of the violin and viola spans the interval of a 4th. Higher positions are also available, but most elementary players concentrate on the first and third positions.

ello and bass The positions on the cello are smaller: from first to fourth finger spans only a minor 3rd, so cellists need to change position more frequently. In lower positions, the double bass player is able to span just a tone from first to fourth finger. Do not therefore write rapid passages for beginners on these instruments.

ouble stops Two (or even three) notes can be played at the same time on adjacent strings within a hand position; this is easier if one of the notes is an open string.

uitable keys Keys which include a number of open strings sound best and are easiest to play. It follows that keys with more than two flats present problems to less experienced players. The really easy keys are G and D.

OPUS

Now write a short solo piece for one of the string instruments. Try to write for a member of your group so that your piece can be played and discussed. Does it suit the instrument? does it sound good? does it lie under the fingers? are there any bowing problems and so on?

Practical guide to woodwind

Sound production

Woodwind players set up vibrations by blowing at a fipple (recorder) or mouth hole (flute) or through a reed (oboe, bassoon and clarinet). These vibrations then transfer themselves to the column of air in the instrument to produce a sound.

Tonguing

Unless the music is slurred, woodwind players tongue each note with a *tu* or *du*.

tu   tu   tu   tu

A slur shows that only the first note is to be tongued, the breath being allowed to flow on through the other notes.

tu _____

Not all notes slur equally well, but in the main, upward leaps are more effectively slurred than downward ones.

tu _____ tu

Articulation

To appreciate the difference in articulation between tongued and slurred notes, a demonstration is necessary. However, some idea can be gained by singing a motive to yourself and 'tonguing it' as if you were playing, like this:

tu   tu   tu   or   tu   tu _____   or   tu _____

Breathing

Woodwind players must have an opportunity to take a breath, so a feel for phrasing their music is important. However, experienced players can play several bars at a moderate tempo in one breath and do not have to breathe after every slur or even at very short rests.

Breathing is not usually marked in the music, but be aware of the necessity for it and do not write lines and lines of semiquaver figures without a breathing space.

tural scale

Each woodwind instrument has a six-note natural scale. Before the introduction of key mechanisms this scale was produced by covering from one to six holes with three fingers of each hand. Accordingly, it is this natural scale and its first overblown higher sounds which are most easily played. The more of these notes you include, the less trouble beginners will have with your music.

recorder in C, flute and oboe   clarinet   bassoon

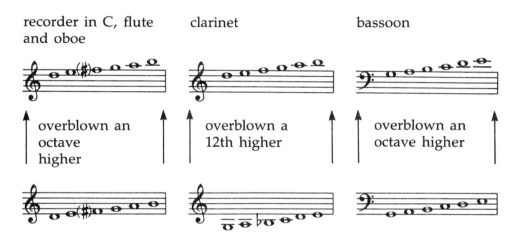

overblown an octave higher   overblown a 12th higher   overblown an octave higher

gered notes

third note is F♯ on recorder and oboe (note also that top A and B less easy to play on oboe)

these are the written notes; clarinet in B♭ sounds a tone lower

In addition to the natural scale, the next note up is also easy to play.

Note that the beautiful lower register of the flute is easily drowned by other instruments, whereas the oboe in the same register comes through clearly.

table keys

It follows from the notes of the natural scale that keys with not more than one sharp will be easiest. Remember however that as the clarinet in B flat sounds a tone lower than written, a piece in C will sound in B flat and a piece in G will sound in F. This does not matter when the clarinet is playing by itself, or with other clarinets, but it does lead to difficulty when the clarinettist plays with other inexperienced woodwind and string players who also prefer easy keys. Except in one case, either they or the clarinettist have to be prepared to play in a slightly more difficult key, as can be seen from this table.

In C	clarinet plays in D	(possible for clarinet)
In D	clarinet plays in E	(hard for clarinet)
In E♭	clarinet plays in F	(easy for clarinet, very tricky for many other limited-ability players)
In F	clarinet plays in G	(a good choice if others know their fingerings for Bb)
In G	clarinet plays in A	(hard for clarinet)
In B♭	clarinet plays in C	(best for clarinet, some other players might be less happy)

Luckily the clarinet being a B♭ instrument combines easily with brass instruments, which prefer flat keys.

Saxophone

Saxophones work like clarinets but are made of brass and therefore combine the qualities of reed and brass instruments.

OPUS

Write a piece for flute or clarinet. Find someone to play it for you. Ask them whether it is well written for their instrument.

Practical guide to brass

Tone production

Brass players produce tone by vibrating their lips within a mouthpiece. These vibrations are then transferred to the tube of the instrument. The length of tube is changed by valves or a slide. By varying the tension of the lips, the player produces a series of notes at each of the seven lengths of tube.

guing

Unless the music is slurred, brass players tongue each note. As with woodwind, the choice of tongued and slurred notes adds vitality to the articulation. For rapid passages, especially of repeated notes, more advanced players employ double (or triple) tonguing, thus: *tk tk* or *tkt tkt*.

athing

Brass instruments use up more breath than woodwind, and this must be remembered when you write for them. Give players plenty of rests, and they can then get their breath back and ease their lips from the pressure and vibration. Brass players talk about 'losing their lip' when it won't vibrate.

ural notes

The easiest and purest sounds on a brass instrument are those which arise from the fundamental length of the tube, without the use of valves or slides. As all brass instruments except the trombone are transposing instruments, the natural notes are those written in the key of C. They are the notes of the harmonic series, picked out by the tension of the player's lips.

trumpet in B♭   horn in F   trombone

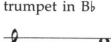   

These are written
notes; the trumpet
in B♭ sounds a tone
lower.

These are written
notes; the horn in F
sounds a perfect 5th
lower.

These are the actual
sounds at 'concert
pitch'; the trombone
is not a transposing
instrument.

The fundamental sounds are lowered by opening a valve or extending a slide. The first valve lowers the sound a tone, the second valve a semitone, and the two valves together lower the sound a minor 3rd. The third valve lowers the sound by a tone and a half. Trombone slide positions are similar. Brass players have to listen all the time to correct their tuning and the problems of playing in tune increase when the third valve is used. When just the first two valves are used the trumpet and horn can play the following *written* notes, although in practice it is best with beginners to keep to the bracketed range.

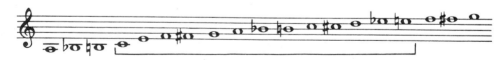

The first four positions of the trombone slide give the same range of notes a 9th lower.

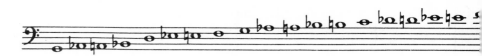

The top of the range requires a tighter lip and is less easy. It is usually written in the tenor clef to avoid leger lines. Notice the gap between the fourth and fifth notes in both ranges. This arises from the non-use of the third valve.

Suitable keys

Because the instruments are pitched in B flat or F, flat keys are preferred to sharp keys.

Modified tone

Horn players put their right hand in the bell of the instrument to adjust the pitch slightly. Before the invention of valves, this technique was necessary to obtain some notes of the scale. If the hand is inserted far enough to close the tube, the sound is muted and, because the length of the tube is shortened, is also a semitone higher. These stopped notes have a special effect.

Trumpets and trombones use mutes to modify the sound in various ways, but whereas the horn player can change instantly (if necessary in the middle of a note), time is needed for other players to put the mute in or remove it.

Brass band instruments

The various instruments of the brass band have the same basic characteristics as the orchestral brass and are most at ease with the suggested range and keys. Some are B flat instruments which sound a tone, or a tone and an octave (or two), lower than written; the remainder are E flat instruments sounding a minor 3rd higher or a major 6th (plus an octave for the bass) lower. Except for the trombone, all brass band instruments are notated in the treble clef; this makes reading easier for the majority of players and allows a player to move from one instrument to another without trouble.

OPUS

Choose a brass instrument (preferably one which is available in your group). Write a duo for it, with either a percussion instrument or another member of the brass family. Be sure to show the articulation clearly with slurs and dots. Remember to give the player a rest or two.

Practical Guide to Percussion

Sound production

Percussion instruments are so called because to make a sound they must be hit or shaken. It is important that the hand, stick or beater rebounds, allowing the instrument to vibrate and sound. Many percussion instruments make only a short sound, but others resonate for a while and have to be damped with the hand or fingers when the sound is to end.

Sticking

Timpani and the keyboard percussion are played with a basic 'hand to hand' technique of alternate hands. When composing for these instruments, keep this left–right action in mind. Occasionally crossovers or double beats are used to simplify a passage which otherwise might tie the player in knots! Snare drum playing makes use of the very lively bounce from the batter-head and a 'mummy–daddy' technique of LLRR is used.

Common figures

Percussion music makes great use of the following figures:

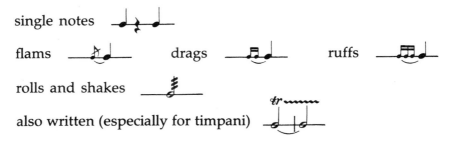

Drags and ruffs are a feature of snare drum parts but are written for other instruments as well. A single shake on a tambourine is easy for most people; a snare drum roll requires a great deal of skill.

Dynamic range

Most of the percussion family have a great dynamic range. Be sure t mark your parts carefully from *ppp* upwards.

Tonal variety

Except for tunable drums and keyboard percussion, the instruments of this family have a limited pitch range, but most instruments have a wide range of colour according to the way they are played. Players use fingers, hands or knuckles to strike the instrument and a range of beaters from small to large and from soft to hard, as well as other objects like coins and knitting needles. The side drum can be played with or without snares and the player can slip in a rim-shot for added variety.

Chief types

Keyboard percussion e.g. glockenspiel, xylophone
Instruments to be struck e.g. gong, triangles, cymbals
Instruments to be shaken or scraped e.g. castanets, maracas, sandpaper blocks
Drums e.g. snare drum, bongos, timpani

OPUS

Write a piece for three percussion instruments. Use three players or arrange the instruments so that they can be played by a one-man band. Remember to show dynamics clearly.

Practical guide to the piano

Sound production

The strings of a piano are struck by felt hammers. The sound continues while the key is held down, but fades all the time. When writing for the piano, take this into account by not writing long note unless they are supported by moving patterns underneath. Even then it is better to break them up with repeated and decorative figures.

ourite figures

A great deal of keyboard figuration is designed to lie under the hands in such a way that it can be easily repeated. Other figures, such as extended arpeggios, require a change of position, in which the thumb is passed under the hand or the fingers over the thumb. Here are a few of the figures you will find in keyboard music.

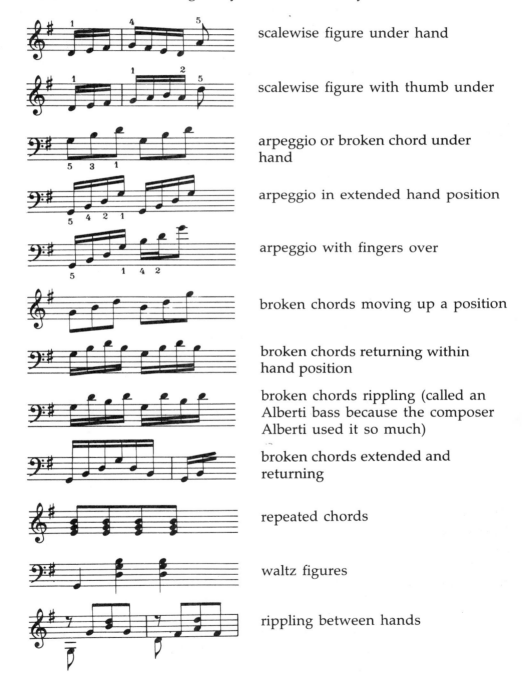

scalewise figure under hand

scalewise figure with thumb under

arpeggio or broken chord under hand

arpeggio in extended hand position

arpeggio with fingers over

broken chords moving up a position

broken chords returning within hand position

broken chords rippling (called an Alberti bass because the composer Alberti used it so much)

broken chords extended and returning

repeated chords

waltz figures

rippling between hands

Range

The piano has a range of just over seven octaves. Apart from the stretch and perhaps the difficulty of reading the notes, it is no hard to play in an extreme octave than it is in the middle. Make use of t different effects which can be had from high passages, low passages, widely spaced hands and close hands.

Articulation

Sounds can be joined (legato) or separated (staccato) or any degree between. As with other instrumental families, use articulation to the full to present your ideas.

Pedals

The piano has a sustaining pedal (the 'loud' pedal) which holds on to the sound by allowing the strings to vibrate undamped. It is used t join up chords and notes which cannot be joined with the hands ar for building up the texture by sustaining some sounds while new ones are added.

There is also a soft pedal (called the 'una corda') which not only softens the sound but also gives it a different quality.

A few pianos have a third pedal which can be used for sustainin particular notes or chords.

Keys

As pianists do not have to form their notes, but only to find them, the range of keys available should be greater. However, many inexperienced players are usually afraid of or unfamiliar with black notes, and so it is safer to keep to easier keys.

Modified tone

Recent composers have experimented with the sounds which can be found in the inside of a piano. The strings can be strummed like those of a harp, or plucked, or hit with beaters. Sometimes the strir are 'prepared' by attaching screws and wedges to them. The range tone colour is greatly increased by such means. Access is easier wit a grand piano.

OPUS

A Make up a short piece for piano using some of the figures listed or some which you have found yourself. Use the pedal for building up the texture.

B Make up a piece which uses the inside of the piano for its sound source. Think up a suitable way to write down strums, beatings and so on.

Practical Guide to the Guitar

Sound production

The sound is produced by plucking or strumming the strings. The sound is increased by the body of the instrument in an acoustic guitar or by electrical means.

Notation and range

The guitar has a range of about three-and-a-half octaves upwards from E.

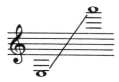

It is notated in the treble clef, but sounds an octave lower than written. The guitar is also written in various tablatures which show not the notes but the position of the fingers in both left and right hands.

Right-hand figures

The right hand can pluck single string melodies or figures with the thumb (lower three strings) or the fingers (upper three strings).

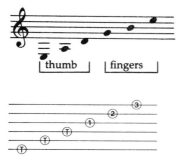

The right-hand fingers are traditionally labelled with initials derived from the Spanish and French words.

p	i	m	a
pulgar	índice	médio	anulár
thumb	index	middle	ring

You will often see these letters in guitar music but here the thumb is labelled T and the fingers 1, 2 and 3.

Favourite figures include

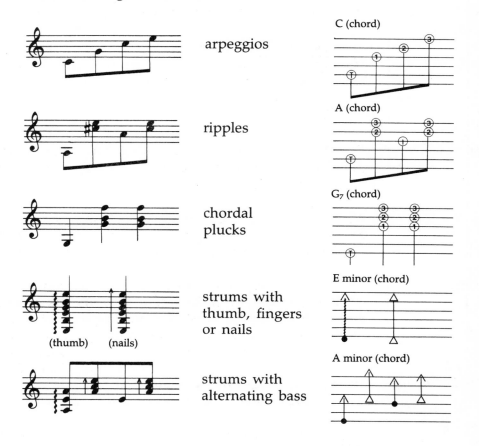

arpeggios

C (chord)

ripples

A (chord)

chordal
plucks

G₇ (chord)

strums with
thumb, fingers
or nails

(thumb)   (nails)

E minor (chord)

strums with
alternating bass

A minor (chord)

Left-hand position   The left hand stops or shortens the strings to make higher sounds. It
stops them just behind a fret. Each hand position covers four frets or
semitones. For instance, in the first position these notes can be
played on the six strings:

and in the fifth position these notes are available.

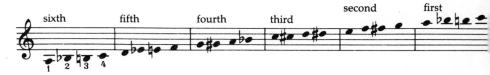

As with bowed string instruments, dropping down to the open string is possible from any position.

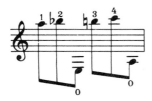

onal variety

The tone of the guitar can be varied, according to the point at which the string is plucked. The nearer the bridge the harder the tone, the nearer the fingerboard the mellower.

eys

Keys which include a number of open strings (especially the three lowest) are easier to play and more resonant. Therefore the keys of E, A and D major and minor are the favourite guitar keys.

Modified tone

The player can drum on the body of the instrument with the fingers, or slap the bridge with the side of the hand, as well as pluck the strings closer to the bridge or to the fingerboard. Electric guitars modify the sound in a number of striking ways including vibrato and tremolo; reverberation and echo effects; and fuzz, where the top frequencies are cut, giving an almost 'square' sound.

OPUS

Either write a guitar accompaniment to a tune you know already or write a short solo piece for guitar. Use the figures given or make up some of your own. Be sure to choose an easy key. Try to have the piece played and discuss it with the instrumentalist.

7 Musical journeys

What is usually called 'form' in music is really like a journey in sound. The music sets off with an idea or two. It repeats them, turns them over, lifts them up, puts them down, hides them or extends them in some other way. It may collect up a few contrasting ideas which it plays with for a change as it makes its way onward. When it arrives, it may be so pleased with its new surroundings that it shows of all or some of its ideas in different ways, becoming more excited as i does so. Suddenly, it realises that it should start its journey back. It bundles up everything and sets off. As it returns homeward, it rearranges its first ideas into their original places and if it does not give the new ideas back, it finds places for them as well. Like all well-organised travellers, it arrives on time!

Think about this journey.

It has unity: the first idea or two are taken on and treated in different ways and places.

It has repetition: both of ideas and of journeys (i.e. there and back)

It has variety: the ideas are rearranged in different ways and shown off.

It has contrast: new ideas are collected up and the music visits another place.

It has balance: the outward and inward journeys are similar, ever if coming home seems quicker.

It has shape: the journeys are each side of the visit and the ideas are settled in or returned.

It has a climax: as the ideas are excitedly mixed up and compared and as the moment to go home arrives suddenly.

It has scale: as it arrives on time and no part is too long in comparison with another.

These are all important elements in any musical form.

So that they are easy to talk about, musical forms are given names. Sometimes they are labelled as well. This allows us to have, at a glance, a bird's eye view of the form, but it must never be forgotten that in music, form unfolds in time, whereas in a picture it unfolds in space. Let the forms be like a map for your journeys, but do not be afraid to explore a few byways of your own.

three-part or ternary form

This is like a simple version of the journey described at the start of the chapter. The music sets out with an idea or two and after a short while arrives at the place it is to visit. There it looks at other ideas in another key, in contrast to the journey music. When it has had enough of these, it takes the same route home. It is labelled A B A.

outward journey	visit	homeward journey
A	B	A
one or two ideas	new ideas	first ideas repeated
home key	away key	home key

Notice

a. the music is the same for both A sections and ends clearly on the tonic in the home key

b. the middle section B is in a different key, which is often the dominant or the relative minor, but may be any contrasting key

c. the middle section uses either new ideas, or, as if it were telling a tale about the journey, ideas which grow out of the first ideas.

Some longer pieces in ternary form have a number of ideas in the first and last sections.

OPUS

Make up a piece of about 16 bars which ends on the tonic or sounds finished in some other way. Now make up another piece, in a different key, which contrasts with the first piece but somehow seems to belong to it. Sometimes this unity is helped by letting an idea from the first piece develop in a different way. Let the second piece be of similar length to the first piece. Now put the two pieces together in a ternary form. There is no need to write out the first piece twice, unless you wish to vary it in some way. Just use suitable words or abbreviations at the end of the second piece to show that the first is to be repeated.

rondo form

A rondo is like a number of day trips, where you set off each day, but return home each night to sleep. Because the music makes a number of visits, it explores a number of other keys. Rondos are a simple extension of ternary form and are labelled A B A C A.

A	B	A	C	A
home key	first away key	home key	second away key	home key

The name rondo means round: the rondo tune keeps 'coming round again'. The visiting B and C sections are sometimes called episodes. A rondo may have a short tailpiece or coda at the end to round things off, as if it were discussing the visits.

OPUS

Write a short lively tune or piece which will be good to hear three o more times. Then write two other contrasting tunes which will go together with the rondo tune. Choose different keys for each episode, for instance dominant and relative minor.

Variation form

Variation form is like making the same journey several times, but each time travelling in a different way.

You could walk

or dawdle

or run

or bus

or bike

or go in other ways.

Notice

a.   the simple outline of the first walking tune which in a set of variations is called the theme

b.   the way the outline of the tune can be traced in each variation

c.   that each variation is different and in contrast to the others.

The theme or tune for variations must have a clear shape or harmony, so that it is easy to recognise when it is decorated and changed in other ways. Each variation might show a change of mood, tempo, rhythm or key, or be decorated with extra or repeated notes. The texture might be thinned or thickened, or the articulation varied by the use of staccato or slurs. The variation might be changed in colour or instrumentation. Whatever happens, the outline, basic idea, phrase structure or harmonic framework should always be present in some way. The one exception is in the last variation which sometimes goes off freely to form a coda.

Early sets of variations were called divisions because they divided the tune up into ever smaller notes. A special form of variation is one where the tune first comes in the bass and is repeated over and over again while the parts above are varied and extended. This is known as divisions on a ground (bass).

OPUS

Find or make up a short tune or piece of between 8 and 16 bars. Make sure it has a clear shape and is easy to spot when it is changed. Write a number of variations on it.

Two-part or binary form

Binary form was very popular in 17th- and 18th-century music but has been less used since those times. As its name suggests, it is in two parts. In the first, the music journeys away; it modulates to the dominant. Then the second part starts in the dominant and makes its way home, modulating back to the tonic. Both parts are usually repeated.

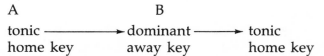

A   B

tonic ——————→ dominant ——————→ tonic
home key   away key   home key

Because the second part spends time in the dominant (and perhaps other keys), it is quite often longer than the first part.

Some binary pieces have two or more groups of ideas. The second group often arrives at the same time as the move to the dominant (in the first part), and the return to the tonic (in the second). The last few bars of each part are often exactly the same, but in different keys.

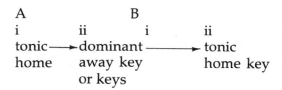

A   B
i   ii   i   ii
tonic——→dominant ——————→ tonic
home   away key   home key
            or keys

For full effect, binary form depends on this very clear key structure. This may be why it has been less in fashion since the 18th century. Look at pieces in binary form by Bach and Scarlatti and follow their journeys in sound. They are fine models for your own pieces in this style.

Organic or free forms

Some forms, like melodies, grow organically. Each section grows out of the previous one as the piece develops. These forms are sometimes linked to a story. The principles of unity, contrast, variety, repetition, shape and climax must still be applied, otherwise the music may ramble on aimlessly to nowhere.

Some forms grow freely. Section is added to section as the piece grows. The sections are sometimes sharply contrasted so that the piece gains strength from opposing forces as they press against each other. Many rhapsodies are in free forms of this nature.

You will find many opportunites to write in these forms in the following chapters of this part of the book.

8 Words and music

Words and music are linked together in four ways.

a. Where the words themselves are spoken or recited with the rhythms, pitch changes and varied colours of music. The scat word ideas at the start of this section were treated in this way.

b. Where the words are read or spoken over or between music, which may follow more or less closely the sense of the words.

c. Where the words are semi-sung on approximate pitch levels and the voice is used in a variety of ways to produce special effects. Such vocal effects are used both with and without electronic and other instruments.

d. Where the words are set in a traditional manner to a melody which may be for solo, group or chorus. The voices may be accompanied or unaccompanied.

These four ways might merge and combine with each other; for instance, words might be recited rhythmically above an instrumental background or speech-song move into pure song and back again.

As, even today, the most common association of words and music is in song, this will be looked at first. Here are the main stages in setting a poem to music.

•ng

a. Choose a poem which is direct in its appeal and seems to need music. Here is a poem by John Scott which I like: it has a message for all time and lends itself to music.

> I hate that drum's discordant sound,
> Parading round, and round, and round:
> To thoughtless youth it pleasure yields,
> And lures from cities and from fields,
> To sell their liberty for charms
> Of tawdry lace, and glittering arms;
> And when Ambition's voice commands,
> To march, and fight, and fall, in foreign lands.
>
> I hate that drum's discordant sound,
> Parading round, and round, and round:
> To me it talks of ravaged plains,
> And burning towns, and ruined swains,
> And mangled limbs, and dying groans,
> And widows' tears, and orphans' moans;
> And all that Misery's hand bestows,
> To fill the catalogue of human woes.

b. Read through the poem and decide which words or syllables are accented. Mark them with a tick or line.

　　 ✓　　　　 ✓　　　 ✓　　　　 ✓
I hate that drum's discordant sound,

　　　 ✓　　　 ✓　　　　 ✓　　　 ✓
Parading round, and round, and round:

　　Any of these might be set at the beginning of a bar, while unaccented words will come on weaker beats.

c. Space out the words. Then think of rhythms which will fit them and the mood of the poem. Write the rhythms above the words. Use one note to a syllable unless you are sure a word needs to be given a number of sounds in the form of a melisma.

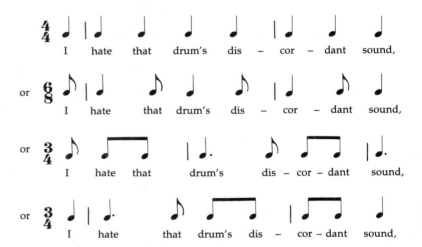

The first two rhythms are dull and regular. The third seems better, but the last has more life and variety. The quavers across the bar-line push it on and the words that seem to me important are stressed at the beginning of the bar.

d. Set the words out under a stave with the rhythm above. Draw in the bar-lines and leave space between the clef and time signature for any sharps or flats you may need to add.

e. Try to think of a tune for this phrase. If the song is to have an accompaniment, it will be better, at this stage, to have in mind a few chords or clusters, so that the tune can move more easily, 'hand in hand' with the progression. Write them with letters or

Roman numerals above or below the stave. Now dot in the tune on the stave.

f. Before adding the stems and beams to the notes, make any changes you wish to the pitch or rhythm; for instance, what about strengthening 'hate' with a melisma?

Now with a leaning note added, the singer will be able to make more of the word. Notice the slur above the notes and the short line after the word to show that it is set to more than one note.

OPUS

If this poem appeals to you, complete it in your own way. Keep in mind what was said about 'writing a good tune' in chapter 3. An accompaniment can be outlined as the tune grows, or alternatively added at the end. Chords and clusters may be suitable, or a single line or a melody or percussion instrument may be more appropriate. For this, the work you did in Partnerships will be of help.

If you do not like this poem, or think it unsuitable for setting, find one yourself, or make one up, and set it to music in a similar way.

**peech-song
nd vocal
ffects**

Speech-song and other vocal effects can be merged with traditional song or used by themselves. They are often found in more experimental music, where timbre, dynamics and texture are just as important as pitch and rhythm. They are equally effective in solo or chorus. New vocal effects are constantly being invented and the notatation even of well-tried sounds is not yet universally agreed.

Here are a few examples of the more frequently heard vocal effects. You may like to experiment with them and find others for yourself. All can be modified further by electronic means. Their relative pitch can be shown on one, three or five lines as here:

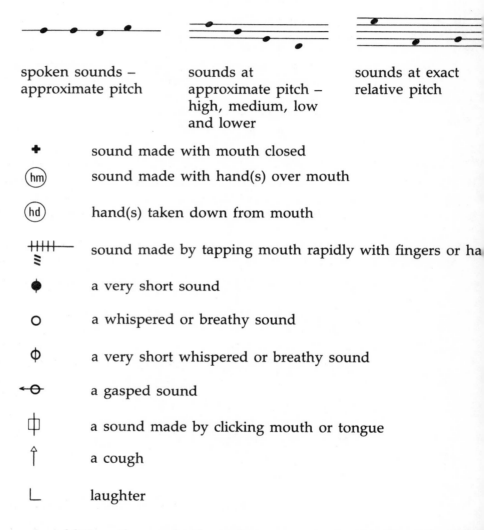

spoken sounds –
approximate pitch

sounds at
approximate pitch –
high, medium, low
and lower

sounds at exact
relative pitch

+   sound made with mouth closed

(hm)   sound made with hand(s) over mouth

(hd)   hand(s) taken down from mouth

╫╫╫   sound made by tapping mouth rapidly with fingers or ha[...]

🔸   a very short sound

○   a whispered or breathy sound

ɸ   a very short whispered or breathy sound

←○   a gasped sound

⊕   a sound made by clicking mouth or tongue

↑   a cough

∟   laughter

In addition, the words themselves are sometimes split up into the[...] individual syllables or even letters.

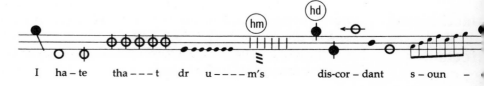

I   ha – te   tha – – – t   dr   u – – – – m's   dis-cor – dant   s – oun   – [...]

OPUS

Continue this poem in a similar manner using the vocal effects to strengthen the impact of the poem on words like 'thoughtless youth', 'lures', 'tawdry', 'widows' tears' and 'Misery'.

Alternatively, find or write a poem or words of your own which you think will lend themselves to use in this way.

Music and the spoken word

Poetry which may not lend itself to setting traditionally or experimentally may still be enhanced by being linked with music. (Prose readings may be treated in the same way.) The music may be performed at the same time as the reading, or between verses, sections or individual poems. It may be vocal or instrumental, traditional or experimental. It may closely follow the sense of the reading by being timed to coincide with certain words or phrases, or it may just reflect the mood more generally and remain in the background until the poem has been read.

'The Drum' could be treated in this way with a solo reciter or chorus with instruments. A simple option might be to make up a piece of music using drums of different sorts and sizes. Alternatively, a drum-like rhythm on guitars or strings might be more imaginative to start the music, drums themselves being saved for an interlude between the verses after the words, 'To march, and fight, and fall, in foreign lands.' Voices too could produce drum-like sounds or they might be reserved for a coda or postlude at the end of the poem; there is plenty in the second verse to suggest their use.

Remember these points when writing music to go with the spoken word.

a. Do not let the music drown the voice. One solution may be to amplify the voice; otherwise select background instruments and effects carefully.
b. Do not upset the balance by improvising or writing music which takes up too much time before, between or after the text.
c. Set the mood as simply as possible, but use your imagination to avoid obvious and cheap effects.
d. Allow plenty of repetition in the music so that it does not detract too much from the words.

e. If certain words or passages are to be linked directly with music, then careful timing of both text and music will be necessary in rehearsals. It is usually a good idea to include a bar or two which can be repeated ad lib while the speaker catches up.

OPUS

Write music to be linked with 'The Drum', or find another poem or text which would be effective when spoken surrounded or accompanied by instrumental or vocal music.

Word music

Words can be chosen and then repeated, fragmented and grouped for their own effect. As with scat words, they may not make sense, but make their appeal in sound direct. Alternatively, phrases may be selected carefully for their emotional impact and meaning. The words can be repeated with metrical rhythm or said in free time. They can be raised or lowered in pitch even though they are not sung. The quality of voice or timbre can be changed, as can the dynamic level. Their delivery can be broken up with silences. They can be passed from one group or soloist to another as phrases, words or fragments. They can be spoken in blocks of sound or in canon and counterpoint. Group can echo group, and voice can be piled on voice in a textural crescendo.

As with other ways of linking words and music, word music can be joined with song, vocal effects or instrumental backgrounds.

OPUS

Find words which you would like to present as word music or use the poem 'The Drum' in this way.

9 Descriptive music

Ready-written and recorded mood music can be selected and bought by film and television producers. It is an alternative to music specially commissioned from a composer for a particular production. Like ready-made clothes, the music may not fit perfectly. But it does have the advantage that it can be heard in advance by the producer; and it is cheaper!

As its name suggests, mood music creates a mood:
down in the dumps, on top of the world, worried, angry or loving;

but it can also paint a picture:
a lakeside scene, a clattering factory, a gloomy prison cell;

or heighten an action:
a buzzing mosquito, a car chase, a flight to the moon;

or capture the feel of the weather:
an icy morning, a stormy night, a blazing desert sun.

As you can see, composers of mood music need to use their imagination. They also have to use their skill in choosing the right instruments for their ideas and in presenting those ideas so that they have the right effect on the producer and audience.

I expect you already have some ideas for mood music yourself, but before starting to write or improvise ask yourself these questions.

What mood am I trying to set?
What does it feel like to be depressed, or under a blazing desert sun or in a car chase?
Will a good tune (with or without an accompaniment) give the right feeling?
Or would it be better to have something repetitive or rhythmic?
What about some exciting and unusual chords in unexpected progressions?
Or some experimental sounds which just hang in the air?
Would a thin sound or a rich texture suit the mood?
Would well-placed silences help to raise the tension?
Which instruments shall I use?
Or would voices be more effective?
Could I record and then modify natural sounds?
Would other electronic effects be better?
Should I try to imitate the sound of a car exactly?
Or would it be better just to capture the urgent rush of the engine and roar of the tyres and let the music grow out of them?

What about the shape of my piece?
Should it be constant or should it grow towards a climax?
How long should it be?
How will I make it possible to extend or reduce it to fit the action i
  necessary?

When you have answered some of these questions you will need
to make up your mind whether to write the piece out for yourself
and others to play, or to improvise. Even if you improvise (especially
in a group), you will probably need to provide some prompts or
framework. If your music is largely experimental, you will need to
use, or invent, suitable signs and set them on a time scale.

Search your imagination for good ideas and then be sure that the
sounds you are making with voices or instruments are just what yc
want. Do not be afraid to rewrite or try other arrangements of note
instruments or textures.

OPUS

Think of a mood, scene, action or atmosphere for which you woulc
like to make up a short piece. Select instruments or voices which a
available in your group. Remember the strengths and weaknesses o
the players in the group when you are writing, or planning your
improvisation. When your piece has been rehearsed and developed
make a recording so that it is on hand for others to hear and use.

Your mood music could be linked with improvised drama or min
or perhaps with puppets. Look out for opportunities in your school
or club for creative co-operation. Try to encourage others to use
home-made mood music in their productions.

Programme music

Mood music is written to be used as a background to film or drama
Other descriptive music is to be listened to by itself. For hundreds
years, composers have written instrumental and orchestral pieces
which describe or draw their ideas from the scenes and sounds of
the sea, the town and the countryside. Some take a single idea (like
a bird call) and use it as a starting point. Others take a broader loo
at the scene and draw on a wider range of sounds and ideas,

weaving them into the musical fabric. Both might reflect the feelings of their subjects, for instance a sad bird, an angry sea or the feelings of someone in the 'picture'.

Here are some typical titles drawn from the last three hundred years. They may give you some ideas.

Le coucou	Daquin	(a rondo in which the cuckoo call is present nearly all the time)
La poule	Rameau	(a chicken clucks repeatedly)
Les petits moulins à vent	Couperin	(windmills)
Symphony no.6 (Pastoral)	Beethoven	(included in the five movements are peasants merrymaking and a storm)
Au lac de Wallenstadt	Liszt	(a lakeside scene in Switzerland)
La mer	Debussy	(three movements about the sea in its different moods)
Cockaigne overture	Elgar	('In London town', the home of the Cockneys)
Tapiola	Sibelius	(a brooding, dark, mysterious forest in Finland)
From the Diary of a Fly	Bartók	(a buzzing, irritating fly)
Sunday Morning	Britten	(a fine sunny day, with church-bells ringing, from Four Sea Interludes)

OPUS

With the instruments you have available, make up a short piece about one of these titles which will be good to listen to by itself.
Improvise, or write it down in traditional or experimental notation.
Ask yourself similar questions to those you asked about mood music, but be even more careful to get just the right answers for the sounds you need. Shape the piece into a balanced form, perhaps with a climax towards or at the end.

Alternatively, think of other scenes or sounds with which you are familiar and let them spark off musical ideas to be turned into a piece.

Although the music of a piece like the *Cockaigne* overture, with its Cockneys, street urchins, lovers and marching bands, illustrates its subject from several viewpoints, it does not tell a story. However, a great number of famous pieces, like *The Sorcerer's Apprentice* and *Till Eulenspiegel*, do tell a story. In them, we can follow the moods and adventures of the main characters as the story unfolds in music. Pieces like this are called symphonic poems or tone poems and although they can be enjoyed just as music, it is easier to appreciate their shape and structure, as well as their moods, if we know and follow the story.

As with all descriptive music, you need to use your imagination to the full if you are to make up music which tells a story. There is no difficulty in wondering what to do next, as the story will carry you on. You do need to be careful that the music does not just ramble on without sense and purpose. Here are some guidelines to keep in mind when you write story music. A character need not be a person; it might be a bird, a train, or anything else.

a. Search for striking ideas for the main characters or events. An idea might have a catchy rhythm, or a vivid instrumental colour, or a jagged melodic outline, or dense, brooding chords. The ideas need not be loud, but they must catch the listener's attention and fit the part.

b. Allow time for the ideas to grow so that they are recognisable when they return later in the story. Remember the importance of repetition and organic growth. Help the listener to grasp what is going on as the music moves by.

c. Set scenes as in mood music but allow character ideas to be heard where the story demands. Think of the way an aeroplane moves in and out of clouds, first seen and then not seen.

d. Use variation technique to present the characters in different moods and situations. As with all variations, be sure the theme remains recognisable.

e. Do not be carried away with tiny details unless they are important in the story. The listener may not pick them out and they may lead to confusion.

f. Even though the form will be free and related to the programme, keep in mind the need for repetition, shape and balance as well as climax. It is not necessary to make each episode the same length, as a longer passage may be balanced by, say, three short ones, but do not allow an idea to outgrow its place in the piece as a whole.

OPUS

In this programme, D G A has many different feelings about a space voyage. Make up music which reflects those feelings and illustrates the stages of the journey. There will be plenty of contrast in the sound pictures you create, but D G A should be recognisable in the varying conditions. Shape the music to an extended climax somewhere towards the end, choosing the place where you think this might be best.

pace voyage
or D G A

Waiting for blast-off
> How do you think D G A will feel? Try to reflect those feelings in your music.

Upwards into space
> Make the music full of power, but remember how D G A feels: worried, exhilarated?

Weightlessness and sleep
> Perhaps a quieter passage, but with some strange feelings.

Space walk
> Try to evoke the rare atmosphere. A sense of wonder. Maybe a hitch in returning to the craft.

Return and landing
> Re-entry might be very worrying as it is approached. Try to increase the tension if you think this is so, but do not necessarily make the music louder.

Home again
> A great feeling of achievement coupled with relief and joy at being back with the family.

10   Music and dance

Music and dance have been associated for hundreds if not thousands
of years. You can dance without music, but most people find it more
natural and enjoyable to dance with music. It seems to lift them up
and their body moves in sympathy with the sounds. Sometimes
dancers make their own music, either with portable instruments like
castanets, or with bells, shells and other jingles and rattles wrapped
round their ankles and wrists. Sometimes dance music is sung, but
mostly it is played on instruments. In fact the development of
instrumental music from the Middle Ages to at least the Classical
period is clearly linked with the fashionable dances of the time.

Some dances are strongly associated with a particular country: the
jig and Ireland is one example, although jigs ('gigues' in French) can
be found in many countries. Some dances, like the polka in the 19th
century, are associated with particular periods, although they may
remain popular for long after their introduction, as for example has
the waltz. Some dances are associated with religious ritual and
magical rites; the carol was originally a dance. Some dances tell a
story through mime.

Dance and music are really another 'give and take' partnership.
Dance takes the lilt, rhythmic patterns and phrase structure of the
music and turns them into movement, while music takes the grace
and vitality of body movements, detail of steps and physical use of
space and turns them into sound. They both give and take mood and
character which they pass backwards and forwards as one partner
inspires the other.

In folk and traditional dancing, the metre, rhythmic detail and
phrase structure give rise to the mood and character. On the other
hand, in much modern dance and ballet the mood and character
seem to come first and the detail and structure usually follow. Music
and dance is almost a perfect example of the chicken and the egg:
which comes first?

Just for this chapter we will assume that the music comes first, but
remember that if there were no dances, there would be no dance
music. Music for dancing can range from a simple rhythmic figure,
repeated with or without variation, to an imaginative, complex,
electronic experiment. Regardless of type or style, the music should
have one or more of the following qualities:

well-defined mood and character
vital and compelling rhythmic patterns
well-shaped phrase structure.

OPUS

A   A number of dance tunes through the ages have had a drone bass. Of these the musette is the best-known. Its name is derived from a small French bagpipe, which like most bagpipes had a number of drones. The hurdy-gurdy was another instrument which played dance tunes with a drone.

   Make up a dance tune for recorder and viola, or use another pair of instruments, one of which can provide a drone. Let the music have a number of sections, each of four or eight bars. Let the sections be in pairs of similar music with open (non-tonic) and closed (tonic) endings. Use repeat marks with first- and second-time bars to save writing out the music in full.

			1st		2nd		
1	2	3	4 :‖	3	4	:‖	
			open		closed		

			1st		2nd		
5	6	7	8 :‖	7	8	:‖	
			open		closed		

B   The musette was often used for contrast between two gavottes. A number of other dances were traditionally grouped together in pairs, among them the pavan (a stately two beats in a bar) and the more vigorous galliard which were modified in a number of ways to fit the different metres.

   Write a pair of made-up or traditional dances which share ideas. Either write a tune with a drone accompaniment, a piece for two instruments, or a keyboard piece with a tune and simple accompaniment. Keep the phrase structure regular, with open and closed endings to sections.

C   Many folk dance tunes are played on the violin, or fiddle as it is called by folk musicians. The tunes might be played solo, or with a simple accompaniment on the concertina or guitar. In either case, they are based on familiar chords, which change once or twice a bar.

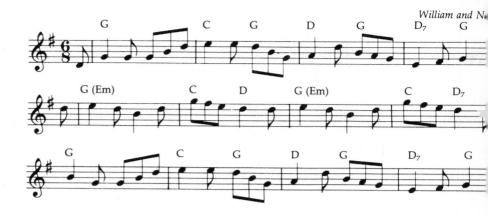

William and Na...

For most folk dances, the tune is repeated a number of times before another tune of similar form is taken up. Write a tune for fiddle or recorder which will go with *William and Nancy*. A change of key might be a good idea. Use a straightforward harmonic framework with a mixture of steps and broken chords in the tune. Accompany with a crotchet–quaver rhythm on the guitar or other instrument. Alternatively, arrange *William and Nancy* for several instruments like this.

D When the waltz and polka were all the rage, a number of different tunes would be strung together for an extended dance. There woul[d] also be an introduction while the couples took to the floor and a coda for a grand finale. Here is the first tune from a polka based o[n] a music hall song by Fred Cape.

The Tin Gee-gee

Fine

D.C. al fine

Notice the accompaniment, which is built on the 'step–step–step–hop' rhythm of the polka. It uses first-inversion chords which are shown with small letters in brackets above the stave. These give a smoother bass line than just root-position chords. The middle section modulates to the dominant before the da capo.

Write another polka tune with four-bar phrases to follow this one. Choose a key other than C or G; perhaps A minor. Your tune could be in contrast to *The Tin Gee-gee*, but must still keep up the 'step–step–step–hop' accompaniment. Write for piano, or for a melody instrument and accompaniment. If the accompaniment is for more than one instrument set it out like this:

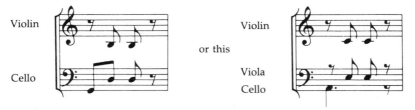

Try writing a short introduction to the first tune and perhaps a coda for a grand finale!

E   Just as the musette originated in France, the pavan in Italy or Spain and the polka in eastern Europe, so in recent times many dances and styles have come from overseas: the fox-trot from black America, the samba from Brazil, the conga from Cuba and reggae from Jamaica.

Like jazz, the music for these dances is often wholly or partly improvised. A chordal framework is agreed or adopted from a tune and the details of the parts are left unwritten. As players and vocalists start to gel, the music is usually recorded. If you have suitable instruments and you know people who can help you develop the skills and subtleties of music like reggae, make up dances in these styles as well.

F   All the projects so far in this chapter have been linked to a particular dance style or form. They have all had a regular pulse which has helped to drive them on. The phrases have been mostly of an even length and have had well-defined endings. They have been traditional and tonal.

Now, in this final project, here is a chance to explore further afield with flowing music which is more flexible in pulse and adventurous in pitch and colour. Your music must still have a definite mood and character, the rhythms must still be vital and compelling, even where they compel the dancers to pause motionless, and the phrase structure must allow the movement in space to be shaped with purpose.

Here, as a scenario for a dance drama or ballet, is *The Weather Forecast*.

> A deep depression off the west coast of Ireland will bring rain and high winds to all areas for the early part of the day. This will be forced away rapidly by strong winds arising from a high-pressure area on the Continent and bringing cooler, brighter weather, followed by a severe night frost.

What sort of sound would you use for a 'deep depression'?
What sort of movement for wind and rain?
What about the conflict between the low- and high-pressure areas?
Which instruments will sound 'brighter'; how will the dancers react to this?
Will the coda be 'stiff' with frost?

Work out your ideas with the dancers, passing ideas back and forth. Improvise, making brief notes as reminders, or write out the music in more detail. Select instruments carefully for the sounds you will require. Might vocal sounds be effective? Consider whether any of the dancers might use small portable instruments like Indian bells.

11   Getting it down

There are three basic ways of making a record of your music. The first is by writing it out in staff or other notation; the second by making notes about the stages of an improvisation; and the third by recording the sound on tape. The first is the traditional method which continues to evolve after many centuries.

**aff
tation**

Music is not notation. Music is sound. Notation is a map of the sound or at least a guided tour to the sound. Music does exist without notation in folk cultures of the world, in jazz and in electronic recordings where they have been composed direct. If everybody had an ear and memory as good as Mozart's, there would be less need for notation. But as it is, musical notation has the considerable value of saving our memory and of giving us the chance to explore and learn unknown music. That value is diminished if the notation is inaccurate, incomplete, illegible or unclear in some other way. This section draws attention to a few practicalities in making a score and, where necessary, parts for your music.

iting the notes

For fair or finished copies, where possible,

use black ink

pencil can be too faint

ball point (although convenient) too messy

felt tip is often too thick and stems
and note heads are too much alike.

Use a music pen nib (which gets thicker
as you press it for the note heads)

Position note heads around lines or in spaces.
Do not overlap a line and a space.
Keep the size even, just smaller than the space
between two lines of the stave.

Keep notes and bar-lines upright.

Make sure note heads are joined to stems on the right (ascending) or the left (descending).

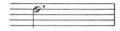

Laying out a score   The score must be laid out in a way which is easy for the conductor to read.

Write names of instruments in full on the first page. Use abbreviations on each open spread afterwards.

Group instruments in families and bracket them at the beginning each system or page. If possible, leave a blank stave between families or use spaced score paper.

Traditionally, woodwind instruments are set out in the highest group, followed by brass and percussion, oddments like piano, guitar, harp or voices and then at the bottom of the page the strings. The instruments within each group are set out with the highest-sounding at the top.

Rule bar-lines vertically, but do not rule between family groups.

Keep beats in line vertically. When setting out, allow space for subdivision of beats.

Add dynamic marks under the stave to which they belong. (If the next stave down has many notes on upper leger lines, write them first before adding marks, to avoid crowding.)

Add tempo marks, rehearsal letters or bar numbers at the top of a system or page. In large scores, repeat the marks at a lower point on the page.

Rehearsal letters or numbers are placed at intervals throughout the piece and are usually in squares B or circles ⑦ . It is most helpful to add them at the start of natural sections, or at places which are likely to need special attention. Bars are usually numbered in fives or tens from the first *complete* bar.

ints on parts

Write out parts as clearly as possible. (Instrumentalists have enough to do without problems arising from badly written parts.) Ten-stave paper is preferable to twelve, as it gives more space between lines for tempo and dynamic marks as well as leger lines. Tempo marks are written above the stave, dynamics below.

Space leger lines evenly above or below the stave. Do not bunch them too tightly.

As far as possible space out crotchets and quavers evenly along the line, allowing a somewhat greater distance for longer notes.

Number bars from the first *complete* bar. Discount any up-beats.

Number bars in fives or tens,

or at the beginning of each new stave.

Add rehearsal letters or numbers if they appear in the score.

Mark whole-bar rests clearly
using rests and figures.

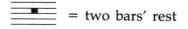

 = four bars' rest    = two bars' rest

Show rests of longer than ten bars like this:

After a rest of more than a few bars, it is
helpful to add a cue from another part before
the player's entry. This might be just a word,

or it might be a few notes, written small
with stems up, just before the entry.
Note the rests for the player under the
cue.

Cues added to transposed parts need to
be transposed as well; here is the same
cue as it would appear in a B flat
trumpet part.

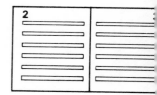

Where parts are longer than one page,
either write out on a spread, for instance on
pages 2 and 3,

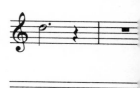

or be sure that the turn arrives as the player has
a bar or two's rest, even if this means leaving
blank staves.

If the player is to start playing straight after
the turn, write 'V.S.' for *volti subito*
(turn at once) after the rest.

V.S

If you intend to have your parts photocopied (you may need several of the same), either use A4 paper or avoid writing in the margins of the manuscript paper. Many small copiers neither take larger paper nor make reductions.

ving time

If it is necessary to save time when writing a score or parts, the following will be found useful.

Repeated groups can be shown like this:

A repeated bar can be shown like this:

Several bars like this:

and a pair of repeated bars like this:

A repeated phrase or section can be shown with double dots. If the repeat is from the beginning, the first double-dotted bar-lines may be omitted.

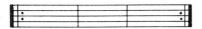

A repeated phrase or section with a changed ending can be shown like this: here the music of the first-time bar is replaced by that of the second-time bar in the repeat.

Where a complete section (as in ternary form) is to be repeated, words or their abbreviations may be added to show a return to the beginning like this:

da capo or D.C.
(from the head)

or a return to a mid-point like this (the sign %% being written in the part or score at the appropriate place):

dal segno or D.S.
(*from the sign*)

If on return the music is to finish before the end of the score or part the word *fine* (pronounced 'feenay') is added where necessary.

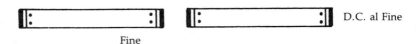

Fine   D.C. al Fine

Extended notation

As composers think of new sounds and combinations, they search for new ways to notate those sounds. Musical notation constantly evolves as existing signs are extended and adapted and new signs are introduced. Here are a few examples which have proved valuable in representing ideas where pitch and rhythm have been used more freely. They might help you to notate some of your music. Make up others of your own, but remember to provide at the beginning of your score a key as to their interpretation. Even some of the signs given here are still little used, so they may be unfamiliar.

Signs for approximate pitch

Use these signs where a passage is so fast that only the overall direction of pitch movement is heard, or where there is so much happening in a dense texture that an individual part only adds to the general effect.

follow contour at a convenient pitch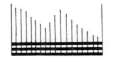

follow contour at about the level shown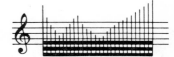

follow contour at about the level shown, moving smoothly; almost like a glissando

↑   high or highest

and

↓   low or lowest notes of instrument or range

slow vibrato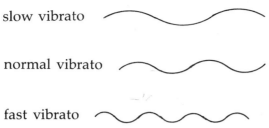

normal vibrato

fast vibrato

rythm signs in
e time

vary length of sound according to spacing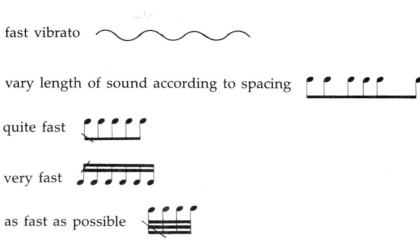

quite fast

very fast

as fast as possible

The next two examples are very useful for freely bending the rhythm in short groups where the use of Italian terms like rall. and accel. is clumsy

get faster

get slower

brief pause ,

normal pause ⌢

long pause ⊓

very long pause ⊡

it repetition

Use these signs where a pattern is to be repeated freely several times.

repeat pattern freely for duration of frame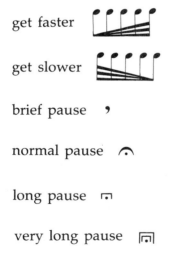

continue the pattern of relative pitch
for length of arrow

repeat sounds freely, starting and ending
on any note (also used without stave)

alternate central note with any other
note or notes (also used without stave)

keep repeating unit until sign is given to stop.

Time scales

To show spacing of sound events in time, write above a time scale
where, for instance, 25 mm is equal to one second

or indicate an overall duration for each section

and/or show the conductor's section down-beats with broad arrows.

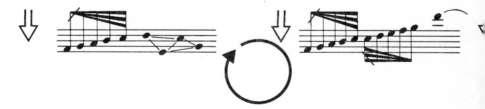

**Memo for
impro**

Improvisation is not necessarily a 'one-off' event, although it can be
Most improvisations are worked on as they are developed and
polished. Where there are a number of players, they interact with

each other in the creation. Sometimes it is helpful to prepare a memorandum as a prompt to the principle landmarks in the piece. The way this 'memo' is written is a personal choice. It will be conditioned in part by the nature, length and complexity of the improvisation. It will be influenced also by what you and the other performers find helpful as a reference. As an example, here is a memo based on an improvisation for the start of *The Weather Forecast*.

Instruments needed (three players)
bass xylophone
various drums, sticks and brushes
tenor recorder
viola
glockenspiel and other high percussion
(arrange so players can see dancers and dancers have space to move)

Start:

low scrubbing on xylo (*pp*)

(watch Vicki for dance cue)

big drum with brush (draw-pat) (*mp*)

(dancers travel to corner)

tenor recorder

vla joins in with quarter tones on C string

(dancers fan out)
(listen for Mark on glock)

clusters on glock (*mf*)

and so on.

Notice in this dance drama that instrumentalists watch the dancers for cues and the dancers listen for cues as well.

Making a recording

By tape-recording your improvisations and compositions you are able to build up a file in sound of your work. Such a record in sound is valuable to you in judging whether the sounds produced are the sounds you wanted. It is valuable to others in assessing your progress and as a complement to your scores and memoranda. The better the quality of the recording, the greater value it has. Here are a few precautions which may help you to achieve a satisfactory result.

Make sure the recorder heads are clean.

If using a cassette, be sure that there is no slack and gently wind tape on to reel before starting.

Run the recorder for a few moments before recording to ensure it is running smoothly.

Match controls to type of tape.

If the level controls are manual, set them so that there is no overloading by checking them against the loudest parts of your piece.

If possible, choose a time when the school is reasonably quiet: not playtime, for instance.

Arrange blankets etc behind performers to damp unwanted echo. Position microphone or cassette recorder away from louder instruments and do not stand them on a vibrating surface like a table top. Be careful not to record over something you wanted to save!

If there is a pause control, use it to avoid unnecessary fuss and clicks when starting to record. Ideally, have someone else in charge of the recording if you are directing or performing yourself.

If there is time, make more than one recording while you have the players there and then choose the best.

Log details of the recording:
work recorded
performers
place
date
position on tape
Dolby yes or no

Switch off and clear up!

Performing section

Contents

Before you play

Except for some electronic music, before it can be heard music must be played. Before music can be played it needs to be prepared. Preparation involves planning and practice.

Planning

Here are some questions to ask yourself when planning a performance for a concert or examination.

When is the performance to take place?
  How much time do we have before that date to learn the music?
Where is the performance to take place?
  In a church, a school hall, a small room, outdoors?
Who is to hear the music?
  Parents, the old people's club, an examiner?
How long is the programme to last?
  Three minutes, ten minutes, half an hour, the whole evening?
Who is to play?
  Just me, two or three others, the school band?
When can we rehearse?
  Every evening for 40 minutes, lunchtimes, Saturday mornings?

You may know a piece of music which you long to play to someone. Or you or your group may have written a brand-new piece which you would like to include in a programme. Then some of the answers to the questions will follow from the music you have already chosen. But usually it is easier to answer these questions first so that you are in a better position to choose suitable music for the place, **the people who are to play and hear it, and the time available for performance and practice. Then ask these questions.**

What shall we play?
  Solos, duets, pieces for small or large group, or a mixture?
  Instrumental or vocal pieces, or both?
  Shall they be modern, classical or early? Or can we mix them up?
  Several short pieces or a longer piece?
Shall we have a theme?
  A composer's anniversary, music about the sea, local composers?

Do we know anything already which is suitable?
That piece we played last year, or that super piece in the Grade IV list?
What would go with that?
Something similar, something contrasting or something by the same composer or from the same period which is quite different in mood?
Is the music suitable for the people who are to play it?
Too hard, too easy or just the right degree of difficulty?
This is important, especially when choosing a pair of pieces for an examination.
Is the music suitable for the people who are to listen?
Popular, serious, unusual or experimental?

When you have made your choice, you must think about the material for a performance.

Where is the printed copy?
In the piano stool or the music room cupboard, or is it still to be ordered from the shop?
This can often take a long time, so plan well ahead.
What about parts?
Are there copies for all the players or singers?
At the present time it is illegal to photocopy almost all printed music, although this may change in years to come. An examiner seeing a photocopy may refuse to examine the candidate.
Shall we need to write out parts?

Preparation

Once you have chosen your programme you must start to prepare the pieces. You may already know them and only need to bring them up to a high standard for playing to other people, including an examiner. You may have to learn a quite new piece and then gradually polish it for public performance. Remember that without someone to play it, music cannot be brought to life, so as a performer, you have a very important job.

Here are some tips to improve your practice. (Notice, incidentally, that this commonly used word is spelt with a 'c' when it is a noun but an 's' when it is a verb: 'I do my piano practice' but 'I practise the piano'.)

Routine practice

Regular practice gives the best results. You are able to refresh your mind and fingers about what they did yesterday instead of what you thought they did some time ago.

Before you practise, try to think about what you are going to play. Fix your mind on what was not very good yesterday and aim to put it right.

If you are practising several pieces, decide which needs the most work. Concentrate on this for most of the time.

There is no hard-and-fast rule that can be given for the length of time you should practise. Ten minutes might be enough for a beginner, two hours might be too little for a more advanced player. One rule can be stated: do not just watch the clock to fill in time. It is better to practise hard for a short time than to idle away a full half hour just to say you have done your practice.

When you practise, think and listen; don't just waggle your fingers!

Singing at sight

Singing at sight has uses outside that of helping you to pass examinations. You may wish to sing a part in a chorus or a song. Most musicians need to be able to hear in their inner ear what the music will sound like before they try to produce it with their finger on an instrument. In this way they can play in tune and phrase the music thoughtfully.

Some people sing at sight as if it were no harder than reading a book. To others, trying to sing at sight is a nightmare, especially if someone else is listening. As with everything, the more you practise the easier it becomes. Notation is really a map of the sound, showing whether it goes up or down or stays still. If you follow the steps below, some of the panic may disappear when you are asked to sight-sing.

1   Listen hard to the key chord and first note.
    Repeat the separate notes of the chord in your head by singing
them up and down as an arpeggio, perhaps in sol-fa like this: doh
me soh doh' soh me doh.

2   Try to fix any notes of the key chord which come in the first bar or
so.

3   Look out for repeated notes.

4   Scale passages are easy, but might change direction or leap suddenly.

5   Look out for unexpected leaps.

    If the music leaps, try to think ahead to the second note. Is it a
note of the tonic chord, which hopefully will be in your head? If
not, how near is it? One note above or below?
Do not hurry. Think ahead.

Playing at sight

The ability to read a piece of music at sight has many uses besides that of helping you to pass examinations. When you learn a new piece, you first have to read it through if you are to gain an idea of its overall mood and shape. You may sometimes be asked to accompany another player or a singer and have very little time to prepare the music in advance. Groups of players often like to play through a piece to see what it sounds like. Unless the music has been handed out beforehand, each person will read at sight. Members of an orchestra often find themselves sight-reading a new work at its first rehearsal.

The better you can read at sight, the more enjoyment you will get out of new pieces. As with all skills, the more you practise the better you will become. Here are steps to take as you attempt to sight-read a piece of music.

1   Note the time signature. How many beats in a bar? Does it start on the first beat?

2   Try to hear the rhythm in your head for a bar or two at least.

3   Look at the key signature. How many sharps or flats?

Switch your mind into the right key. If you have practised your scales, your fingers will be itching to get on to the right notes!

4 Look at the overall pattern: mostly steps or leaps, or a mixture?

5 Try to spot any repeated notes, as these often cause problems.

6 Look out for unexpected leaps.

7 Note helpful bow markings and fingerings.

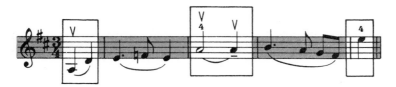

8 Try to feel the shapes under your fingers and the sounds in your head.

9 Look out for accidentals. They last only for the bar in which they occur.

10 Note the tempo etc.

At a moderate pace

Start to play but do not rush.
Look ahead all the time. There may be traps!

Learning a new piece

When you are about to tackle a new piece, look through it as if you were going to sight-read. Note the key, main rhythms, tempo, general shape and so on. Then, however slowly, try to play through the piece with as few mistakes as possible.

When you have done this, look at the piece and try to divide it up into sections. These might be just a phrase or two, or as much as half a page. The advantage of practising a section at a time is that you go through the same music again sooner. If you always tried to play the whole piece, it might be five or more minutes before you went back and started again; when you take a section, it might be as little as 15 seconds before your mind and fingers are working through the same notes again. By this means your mind and fingers will soon find their way round each passage. Keep it all in slow motion at this stage.

It is sometimes a good idea to pick out the hardest parts first. Work at them and then slot them in between other sections. Pianists may need to practise with each hand separately at first. Take care to use sensible fingerings and hand positions. Make use of any fingering or bowing given, unless it really does not suit you. When it doesn't, write in your own (you should always have a pencil handy).

As you get to know the piece, think about what the music is trying to say. Although at first pitches and rhythm must be uppermost in your mind, try to think about details such as articulation: is it staccato, legato or somewhere in between? Do not play the music all at the same dynamic level; introduce some variety as early as possible. Keep playing slowly and gradually add more and more detail.

Once the music is taking shape, start to join up the sections. Do not always begin at the beginning. Sometimes start with a later section and work through to the end.

When you are able to play the piece through without fumbling and breaking down, start to push on the tempo a tiny amount each day or so. It may be weeks before you can play a lively piece up to speed, so do not try to rush the process. Even when everything is flowing smoothly, it is still a good idea to take out some passages for a little extra slow practice. It is also valuable at any stage to do a little 'armchair practice' by studying the piece away from the instrument, thinking it through in your head.

Be patient. By taking care, you will not build in mistakes which can take hours of practice to unlearn.

Rehearsing with others

Many musicians would count playing together in a small group or ensemble the most enjoyable form of music making. You may well find plenty of opportunity to play with others. If so, I expect you too will enjoy the experience. Here to help you are a few points to remember about ensemble playing.

First, if it is at all likely that the music may have problems for some players, try to distribute the parts for practice beforehand.

When you meet to rehearse tune up: if there is a piano in the group, tune to that; if there is no piano (or other fixed-pitch instrument), tune to concert pitch, ideally with the help of a tuning fork or electronic tone. Wind instruments will need to warm up before they can be accurately tuned.

Position yourselves so that everyone can see everyone else. Clean attack in ensemble is difficult enough to achieve, without the added problem of players not being able to see their partners. A large group may have a conductor, but duos, trios, quartets and other small ensembles have to rely on themselves for starts and endings. In rehearsal, counting aloud might be necessary, but this is certainly not possible in performance. A lead has to be given by one player, who must give a preparatory signal by raising the bow, instrument or head in time, on the beat before the start. Then the music begins as the bow makes contact with the string, or the instrument and head return to the playing position. Endings, especially after a long held note, are cut off in a similar way. Players should keep half an eye on each other for bow movements and breathing throughout the piece. It is then easier to judge how long a sound will be held or where a phrase will be rounded off.

Although you might be given a cue or a nod from another player, it is up to you to count rests when you are not playing. This is especially important when the piece is unfamiliar. Several bars' rest is counted like this:

1 2 3 4, **2** 2 3 4, **3** 2 3 4, **4** 2 3 4 and so on.

Decide which piece you will rehearse first, then play it through at an agreed, sensible tempo. As with solo practice, this should not be too fast. If the piece is new, the play-through will help you find out what the piece is about. It will also help you to discover which passages are going to need special attention.

It is usually necessary to 'take out' a tricky passage or section for extra practice. Whoever is in charge should tell the others where it is like this: 'After B – six bars' (not 'Six bars after B').

A tricky passage can often be made easier if the tempo is eased very slightly. This is most helpful when it is difficult for one player to find all the notes up to speed.

As the piece takes shape, consideration must be given to overall balance and to highlighting. Is the piano too loud for the flute? Doe the horn need to play just a little louder to balance the trumpet and trombone? It is sometimes helpful to ask a non-player to help with these decisions, but eventually you must be able to judge from within the group. Sometimes the need is to blend the parts into a rich sonority, at other times one instrument needs to stand out from the others. As with all performance, the ear is the final judge and most music training is, in the end, to do with refining the ability to listen to what is going on.

Directing an ensemble

Many of the points mentioned in the sections on planning and rehearsing with others are relevant to this section. In addition the following should be considered.

Before rehearsal:
Do I really know the music? What is it about? What is it trying to say? Are there any special difficulties?

Study the score in advance, using a coloured pencil to mark such things as changes of time, entries and so on.

At the rehearsal:
Make sure the instruments are in tune with each other.
Make sure you can be seen by everyone and everyone can see you. If the group is large, you may have to stand on something to be see easily.

Be clear in your instructions as to which piece is to be rehearsed and from where you are to start. Select a suitable tempo, so that the music has a chance of being reasonably complete and accurate. As confidence grows and the piece becomes more familiar, the tempo can be increased if necessary.

Give a positive preparatory beat before bringing in the players or singers. In the early stages, it may be necessary to give several beats o counts to set the tempo.

If the music is in strict, regular time, be sure to beat the bars correctly and take particular care to give a good down-beat for the first beat of each bar. Players depend on this to count rests and to keep together. Let the beat flow and move the baton, hand and arm in character with the music: vigorously, lively, smoothly and so on.

Do not feel that you must use both hands in the same way. Reserve the non-beating hand to shape the music and to point up entries in good time to help the players.

If the music is in free time, agree a sign (usually a down-beat, perhaps with both hands) to mark the important points in the music. These may be at timed intervals or, for instance, where there are broad arrows. Give the signs clearly, as players may have to judge their entries from these as well as from other players.

In strict or free time, hold any pauses with an absolutely still hand or baton until the point at which the music is to move on, when a semi-preparatory movement is needed.

Listen hard all the time. Are the players together? Are they playing the right rhythm? Are they playing the right notes? Are any in difficulty? Try not to embarrass them – they may only get worse – but be ready to help. Is the drum too loud? And so on.

It is your job as director to hear what is going on and if necessary to put it right. Do not discourage the players or singers by stopping at the first mistake (unless it causes a breakdown), but remember where it happened so that you can draw attention to it later.

Be enthusiastic (nobody will like the piece if you do not appear to), be encouraging, be helpful, but above all be firm. You will not be able to be firm if you are not sure, so always make certain you know what is in the score. It is an insult to the players if the conductor does not know the work.

The great day

The 'great day' may be a public performance or an examination. Whichever it is you will probably be excited. This is only natural, and if you were not you might give a dull performance. However, try not to become over-anxious or nervous. This is easier said than done, but here are a few tips which might be of help to you.

Try to have a good night's sleep before the day. Try to think of something else before going to bed: what you will wear at the party on Saturday, when the cat will have her kittens, how you will mend that gear on your bike.

Dress appropriately and look as if it is quite an important day. Make sure your hands are clean.

Do not go without breakfast or any other meal. You will need some energy to perform well, so eat something, however little.

Warm up on your instrument before the occasion. Perhaps play through a piece or do a few scales or exercises. This is very important if you play a wind instrument, which will be badly out of tune if it is cold. In winter, keep yourself warm, especially your hands; in summer, try to keep cool, so that your hands are not sticky or slippery. Whatever the time of year, as you wait to go on, try to keep calm by breathing evenly with fairly deep breaths.

Greet your audience or the examiner pleasantly. Neither they nor the examiner are dragons, even if you think they are. Both are there to see how well you can play, not how badly.

If you have not done so already, tune carefully to the piano or other instruments. There is no need to hurry. Take the opportunity to start to feel at home and take a few deep (but silent) breaths. Make sure the seat or music stand is just as you want it and the music is securely placed with any turns prepared by the corner of the page being lightly bent up.

When you and the audience or examiner are ready, start to play. Do not think of them, or of 'poor little you', but think of the music. Make sure those who are hearing it really enjoy it and think it as great a piece as you do! Concentrate on the sounds you are making. Nothing else matters: do not let your mind wander to your party clothes, cat or bike now!

When you have finished, do not just slink off with your tail between your legs. If the audience are generous enough to applaud, face them and seem to say, with a smile and perhaps a bow, 'thank you very much for listening'. If the examiner says good morning, don't just scowl!

Listening section

Contents

Introduction

Before it really exists, music must be turned into sound. That sound must be heard. More than that, unless the music is just for background use, it must be listened to actively. We hear the birds singing, but we must listen more carefully if we are to recognise the songs and calls. It is just the same with music. We must give our attention and engage our ears and minds with the sounds if we are to get the most out of them.

Listening is almost, if not quite, the most important part of music. Composers listen to the sounds in their heads and drag them out, before fixing them into notation or on to tape. Performers listen intently to the sounds they make, not only to hear whether they are in the correct rhythm and at the right pitch, but also to check that they have the right quality and balance with other sounds. Listeners listen to the music and match their mood to the mood of that music as it expresses itself. The more they are in tune with the music, the more it will mean to them and move them.

By listening hard, you will start to hear things you hardly knew existed and gain even more pleasure from music. Perhaps you might also become aware of the sounds around you in everyday life. This might not always be quite so pleasant; but perhaps as a result you will try your hardest to make everyone a little more careful about the noises they and their machines make.

The listening groups which follow in this section will help you to pinpoint some of the ways composers use sound to express themselves. Each group ends with a test, which you will be able to answer on a separate test sheet. These will give you some practice in listening under examination conditions. They may help you to keep a cool head when taking aural tests.

Listening group A

1   Here are three rhythmic introductions. Look at them and then listen to the recording. Which one fits? Write the name of the composer.

b. Allegro   Borodin

c.   Warlock

Which instruments play the recorded example?

2 Use ♩♪ and 𝄾 to write the rhythm of *Waltzing Matilda* in ²⁄₂ time. Write one note to each syllable. The first bar has been done for you.

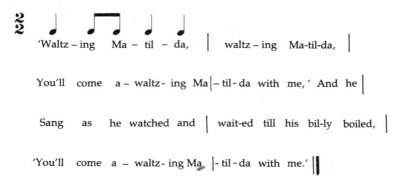

'Waltz – ing   Ma – til – da, | waltz – ing   Ma-til-da, |

You'll   come   a – waltz- ing Ma|– til- da with me,' And he|

Sang   as   he watched and | wait-ed till his bil-ly boiled, |

'You'll   come a – waltz- ing Ma |- til - da with me.' ‖

3 Listen to the lively tune from Janáček's Sinfonietta.
Add stems and tails to these note heads to complete the rhythm.

Three
trumpets

Janáček repeats the tune many times adding an extra two bars every other time.

└────── 3 bars ──────┘ └────── 3 bars ──────┘   +   └── 2 bars ──┘

The first of these is taken up by the cellos and basses and repeated forcefully in sequence three times.

ff

Listen to more of the movement and count the number of times the trumpets play the tune as it is combined with other ideas. Later other instruments take up the tune and play it in different registers, passing it back and forth urgently.

4 Here is the rhythm of part of 'Mattachins' from Warlock's *Capriol Suite*. It follows on from the introduction given at 1c. Listen to the recording and then complete the melody. The first bars of each section have been done for you. Try to spot any bars which are the same and listen hard for repeated notes. The tune moves mostly by step, but there are some small leaps between chord notes. Notice the articulation: slurs and staccato dots show the way the composer wishes the music to be played. Try to add them to your notation.

After this extract, the music is repeated very loudly with a richer texture. It then jumps into a remote key and throws rhythmic chords from one group to another as the music grows in excitement.

Both the *Capriol Suite* and the Sinfonietta were composed in 1926. Peter Warlock was born in London and Janáček in Moravia. Does Janáček's music sound anything like that of other Czech composers, such as Dvořák and Smetana? Try to hear more of these two pieces. They each have a number of movements.

Listening test A

Answer all questions on the test sheet paper provided: questions 1–7 on or under the staves and questions 8–14 in the boxes at the bottom of the page.

Read through the questions. Then listen to the recording. It will be played a number of times with an interval between each playing. As you listen, follow along the staves a bar at a time, pointing with your finger if this helps you to keep your place. A number of bars have been completed and as you follow, the music should be doing what the notes indicate in those bars. Try not to panic.

1 Add the correct time signature after the clef in bar 1.
2 Add suitable dynamic marks under bars 1 and 2.
3 Write the rhythm for bars 3–6 on the note E in the bass clef. The first note is given.
4 Add a rest at the point where the two-bar repeated figure is interrupted.
5 Compare bars 11 and 12 with 13 and 14. What does the melody do? Write the word for this musical device at x.
6 Add a suitable dynamic mark under the stave at bar 19.
7 Complete the music of bars 25 and 26.

8 Which family of instruments plays in bars 1 and 2?
9 What do they play: a rhythm, a tune, a chord or repeated notes?
10 Name two of the instruments which play from bar 3 onwards.
11 How would you describe what happens in bars 19–26?
12 Now listen on from bar 26. What is the same, what is new? Comment briefly.
13 When do you think this music was written: in 1926, about 1810 or about 1700?
14 What do you think it is: a string quartet, a movement of a symphony or a cantata?

Listening group B

1 Listen, several times, to the first section of Chopin's *Grande valse brillante* op.18 no.1. Then copy out the melody adding tails and stems to the note heads given. The introduction, with its surprising cross-accents, has been completed for you. Notice the slight variation in the last line.

a. Which key is this piece in?

b. Where does Chopin use sequences?

c. Where does he stretch intervals on the way towards a climax?

Now listen to the next section of the waltz and describe what happens to the melody.

2 Write the rhythm of the chorus of *Past three o'clock*. One word is set to a pair of quavers, which will be slurred.

Past three o'-clock, And a cold frost-y morn-ing:
Past three o'-clock; Good mor-row, mast-ers all.

3 Here are eight single bars. They are from a minuet in G major by Haydn which has been jumbled up. Listen to the recording several times and then write out the music in the correct order. Add the clef, and the key and time signatures.

When you have shuffled them into the right order, number the bars from one to eight and answer these questions.

a. Does the piece end at the eighth bar? Give one reason for your answer.

b. Which bar is repeated?

c. Which bars are based on the notes of a G chord?

d. What is the third note of bar 1: a passing note, a leaning note or a neighbouring note?

e. Compare the sound of the first four bars with the next four bars. What is different?

f. What is the sign over the minim?

Now listen to the remainder of the minuet. Count the number of bars before the first section returns.

The Haydn minuet was written before 1760, the Chopin waltz in 1831. The Haydn might have been an easy piece for teaching, the Chopin, as its name suggests, a brilliant piece. Think about the keyboard writing in both pieces and make brief comments. Try to listen to some of Haydn's later keyboard music, which is often very exciting in the way it uses the instrument and ideas.

Listening test B

Answer all questions on the test sheet provided: questions 1–8 on c
near the stave and questions 9–16 in the boxes at the foot of the
page.

Read through the questions. Then listen to the recording. It will I
played a number of times. During the interval between each playing
you can start to add your answers. Try not to panic; listen hard,
especially for repeated notes.

1 Add the correct time signature after the key signature.
2 Add a suitable dynamic mark under the first note.
3 Notate bars 3, 4 and 5. There is one rest.
4 Add tails and stems to the note heads in bars 6–8.
5 Add an appropriate mark above the third beat of bar 7.
6 Add the notation to bar 11.
7 Indicate the return of the first tune at the appropriate place by
   writing in the first few bars.
8 Compare bars 5–8 with the last four bars. Then mark with a cross
   the point where the tune changes direction to make for the tonic.

9   Which instrument plays the tune at the beginning?
10 Underneath the tune, the violins are pattering along with a broken-
    chord figure in quavers. Describe what the cellos and basses are
    doing.
11 Which pair of instruments joins in at bar 3?
12 At the start of the middle section (bar 9), the cellos and basses are
    silent. What takes their place?
13 What does the clarinet do when it joins in at the end of bar 10?
14 Which instrument joins in at bar 13?
15 In which key is this piece?
16 Does it ever modulate (or move to another key)? If so, where?

Listening group C

1   Listen to 'Anitra's Dance' from Grieg's *Peer Gynt*. Follow the melodic skeleton below. Then copy the tune into your manuscript book and fill in any missing notes. Start after the introduction, at the upbeat to bar 7. There should be six quavers in each bar from 15 to 20 plus the pair of grace notes in bar 19. Notice the way the intervals in the

♪♪ ♩ ♩ idea are stretched and shrunk. Notice also the way the scale idea grows in the last line.

Now answer these questions about the music.

a.   What is its key?
b.   For which instruments is the piece written?
c.   How do they play in bars 3–6? Which word or abbreviation should be added to the score?
d.   How else is their tone modified? Which words or abbreviations should be added to show this?
e.   Describe what happens in bars 15–18. What is a scale which moves a semitone at a time called?
f.   As in so many pieces, the music modulates towards the end of the first section. Where does it go? What is the name of the key?

2 The tune of *Kum Ba Yah* has been carelessly copied. There are four
mistakes in the melody. Can you spot them? Copy the tune out
carefully in your manuscript books with the mistakes corrected.
Listen to the music in your head!

3 In his Prelude no.7, Chopin uses one two-bar rhythmic pattern eight
times. He changes its melodic shape in a number of ways as the
piece unfolds. Here is an outline of the music with the repeated
notes missed out. Listen to the recording and add these as you write
out the music. The repeated notes in the first, third, fifth and
seventh phrases are all found in the supertonic or dominant 9th
chords; those in the even-numbered phrases are from the tonic chord
and its extension upwards. The chords are printed below the outline
to help you find the notes.

a.   In which key is this prelude?
b.   What does 'dolce' mean?
c.   Which bars are a repeat of an earlier phrase?
d.   Where does Chopin stretch and turn upside down the interval marked 'x'?

Listening test C

Answer all questions on the test sheet provided: questions 1–6 on or near the stave and questions 7–14 in the boxes at the foot of the page.

Read through the questions, then listen to the recording. It will be played a number of times. Use the interval between each playing to add your answers. Keep a cool head. Do not be put off by some slightly unusual harmonic combinations.

1   Add the second phrase, with its stretched interval. Add slurs and dots as in the first phrase.
2   On the first beat of bar 3 there is a glissando. Show by marking it in a similar way the next glissando.
3   Add stems and tails and other suitable markings to bars 8–11.
4   Mark, with two crotchet rests under the stave, the place where the bass accompaniment stops for a moment or two.
5   Mark with an M the point where the music modulates into a bright new key.
6   Add the six missing quavers in bar 15.

7   How would you describe this music: thoughtful, joking, sentimental or urgent?
8   Which instrument plays the tune?
9   Name two of the instruments which play the accompaniment.
10   This melody is made up from three main elements. One is the interval which is stretched at the beginning of many of the bars. What are the other two?
11   Describe what happens around bars 10–12.
12   In which key does the music start and end?
13   When would you say this music was written: is it 17th, 18th, 19th or 20th century?
14   Listen on further. Describe what happens next.

Listening group D

1   Listen to the opening of the Intermezzo Interrotto from Bartók's
Concerto for Orchestra. The oboe tune entirely grows out of the firs
four fierce unison string notes. Until bar 10 it uses just the notes E, F
sharp, A sharp and B, although it uses them at a higher octave. The
first few bars are written out here. Only the rhythm is given for the re
of the tune. Complete the oboe tune by listening to the recording.

   Show the articulation with slurs and dots.
Now listen on further in the movement and compare other
appearances of this tune.

2   Later in this same movement a really good tune is heard, first on th
violas and then on the violins. It is even more varied in its time
changes than the oboe tune at the beginning. Listen to it and then
add stems, tails and dots to the note heads given, to complete the
rhythm in crotchets, quavers and dotted crotchets.

   As with the oboe tune, this melody returns later in the movement
after a very rude and loud interruption to the calm atmosphere.

Listen to the whole movement and notice the appearances of these two tunes.

3 Listen now to another good tune, this time from Smetana's 'Vltava', which is the second in a series of six pieces about Czechoslovakia called *Má vlast*. When you have listened two or three times to the extract, answer the questions below.

a. Do you think the Vltava is a lake, a railway engine, a cathedral or a river?

b. Is the piece in a minor or major key?

c. What is the cadence at bar 8?

d. What device is used in bars 9–16?

e. The tune is played mostly by violins, but there are two bars where other instruments take over. Which bars are these?

f. Which instruments play in these bars?

g. What goes on in the rest which the first violins have at bars 23 and 24?

h. How would you describe what happens when they start again?

i. Compare the shape of the first eight bars of this 'good tune' with Bartók's 'good tune'.

Listening test D

Read through the questions, then listen to the recording, which will be played a number of times. Answer questions 1–6 on or near the stave and questions 7–14 in the boxes at the foot of the test sheet.

1   Write in the first bar of the extract in the treble or bass clef.
2   Mark in a suitable way bars 2–4.
3   Complete the melody in bars 9–11. Bar 10 includes a double-dotted crotchet.
4   Add a suitable dynamic mark in bar 14.
5   Mark with a cross the highest point of the melody.
6   Add to the last bar five quavers and a suitable dynamic mark.

7   Which instruments play the introduction?
8   Which group of instruments plays the tune?
9   How do they play it: in canon, in unison or in close harmony?
10   In what way do bars 9–11 grow out of bars 5–8?
11   Which instrument has the quaver figure at bar 12?
12   What happens to this new idea?
        a. in bars 14 and 15
        b. in bars 16–19
13   Describe the bass line in
        a. bars 1–11
        b. bars 12–20
14   Now listen to the return of this section later in the waltz and describe any changes you hear.

Listening group E

1   Listen to Belinda and the Second Woman singing 'Fear no danger'
from Purcell's *Dido and Aeneas*. Except for the last note of the first
line and one note in the second, they sing all the time in close
harmony a 3rd apart. (Perhaps this shows how much they are in
agreement.) When you have listened to the recording, complete the
music by adding the second part, the rhythmic detail and the bar-
lines. In two places, Purcell raises the lower part with a sharp so that
it leads firmly on to the next note by a semitone.

What are the cadences at x and y?
Listen now to the whole song and notice the way the first line
returns three times in the form of a rondo:

‖: A :‖ B | A | C | A ‖

Now listen to the choral version which follows and notice how
Purcell uses the chorus in relation to the rondo structure.

2   In a powerful passage in the Scherzo from Shostakovich's Fifth
Symphony, four horns play in close harmony. They play two to a
part and, as in the Purcell, are mostly separated by the interval of a
3rd. However, Shostakovich adds vitality and independence by using
other intervals five times, including the first note which is in unison.

Pick out the four other notes which are harmonised with an
interval other than a 3rd. Name the intervals used. Then write out
the passage in close harmony so that you can appreciate the value of
a different melody in the lower part.

3 In the extract from the slow movement of Vaughan Williams's Sixth Symphony, great contrast is made between octave or unison passage and thick chords in 18 parts. As with much of the movement, this string and timpani passage is mostly very soft. It contrasts well with the outbursts and intense, menacing crescendos of other parts of the movement. Listen to this section and then copy and complete the diagram, adding the three textural elements in the right places.

a. 18-part string chords
b. cellos
c. strings in octaves

In addition mark the approximate point at which the timpani join in.

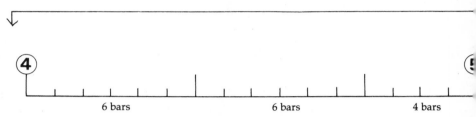

Now listen to more of the movement, which is largely a commentary on war. It is in stark contrast to the pastoral image of much of Vaughan Williams's music.

4 The opening 'Promenade' of Mussorgsky's *Pictures at an Exhibition* is another piece which contrasts unison phrases with chordal passages. Copy out the first 12 bars, then listen to the recording, which is of the original piano version. Write 'unison' or 'harmony' under the music. The change does not always coincide with a bar-line.

a. What is unusual about this music?

b. One bar, from the twelve given, is more thickly harmonised than the others. Which one?

c. Describe the way the music grows from the two ideas in the first bar,

this  and this

If you are stuck, have a look at 'Making an idea grow'.

Now listen to the whole piece. Notice the way the ideas are still taken forward, and listen hard for passages where the music is in unison or octaves.

This 'Promenade' is the prelude to a suite in which a number of pictures are viewed at an exhibition. The first picture is called 'The Gnome', the second 'The Old Castle' and the third 'Tuilleries'. The viewer strolls round, or promenades, between each of these pictures. Perhaps this is why the time is so irregular: when you walk round a gallery, you do so without marching left–right, left–right all the time, but stop and ponder and look this way and that.

Listen now to two more promenades and compare their treatment of ideas. Write a brief description of what you hear.
Consider:

the overall length   (shorter, longer)
the dynamics   (softer, louder)
the register   (higher, lower)
the texture   (thicker, thinner, unison, octaves, chords)
and any other interesting features.

I expect the viewer is musing about what he has just seen, or what has just caught his eye.

If now you listen to 'The Gnome', grotesque and exciting sounds will arrest your attention.

Listening test E

Read through the questions, then listen to the recording, which will be played a number of times. Answer questions 1–7 on or near the stave and questions 8–15 in the boxes at the foot of the test sheet.

1   Add an appropriate dynamic mark below the first note.
2   Add the notation in bar 3.
3   Add the appropriate articulation marks in bars 4–8.
4   Complete the melody in bars 9 and 10 with the correct articulation.
5   Complete the notation in bars 13–16.
6   Add appropriate dynamic marks between bars 16 and 17.
7   Add, under the stave, the rhythm of the accompanying violin and viola parts in bars 21 and 22.

8   In which bar do woodwind and horns first appear?
9   Comment on the instrumentation and texture of bars 9–17.
10 The melody of bars 1 and 2 and 17 and 18 is the same. What is different? Mention three things.
11 Which musical device is used in bars 19 and 20?
12 How do the strings play in bars 21–4?
13 They are marked 'sempre ppp' in the score. What does this mean?
14 Name the cadence in bars 23–4.
15 Now listen on further in the movement and comment on
    a.   the dynamics
    b.   the texture
    c.   the melody
    d.   the harmony, naming the device used.

Listening group F

1   Here is the main tune from the second movement of Berlioz's
Symphonie fantastique. It is entitled 'Un bal' (a ball).

It is repeated immediately with slight variations. Listen to the
recording and then answer the questions.

a.   How many bars' introduction are there before the first complete
bar of the tune?

b.   How would you describe the introduction?

c.   Does this figure go on as an accompaniment throughout the
extract?

d.   Which instruments play the accompaniment?

e.   Why is E sharp written in bar 2 in preference to F natural?

f.   What might the short line between the F sharp and D indicate in
bar 5?

g.   In which bars does Berlioz vary the melody during the repeat?

h.   In the repeat, which word would you add to the music at bar 3?

i.   Which words would you then have to put at bar 5?

j.   Compare the bass line in the original tune with that in the
variation.

Now listen on for a few more bars and answer these questions.

k.   How do the cellos and basses play?

l.   What do they play: chords, scales or scrambled chords?

m.   Which other instrument joins the ensemble?

n.   What does it play?

2 Listen to the start of the third movement of Bruckner's Seventh Symphony.

a. How many times does this motive come before the trumpet enters?
b. How many different notes has the trumpet tune?
c. What goes on underneath the tune?
d. Of what is this an example: a ground bass, two-part counterpoint or variations?

e. Which instruments play this swooping tune?
f. How does it grow?
g. What do the lower strings play underneath it?
h. What happens next?
i. The swooping tune comes again and again. What happens each time it comes?
j. Then another tune enters high on the violins. Is it quite new?
k. If not, where does it come from?
l. What happens to this tune?
m. Write the rhythm of the tune, which lasts four bars.

3 Like the Berlioz, the third movement of Dvořák's Eighth Symphony is in $\frac{3}{8}$. The very singable tune grows by sequence and variation and by being passed from one group of instruments to another. It is mostly built from two-bar phrases. Here is the plan of the phrase structure. Copy it and then listen to the recording. Many phrases have been labelled. Slot in the others from the descriptions printed below the plan. New ideas occur or return at A and B . These are rehearsal letters, which are placed at the beginning of important sections of the score.

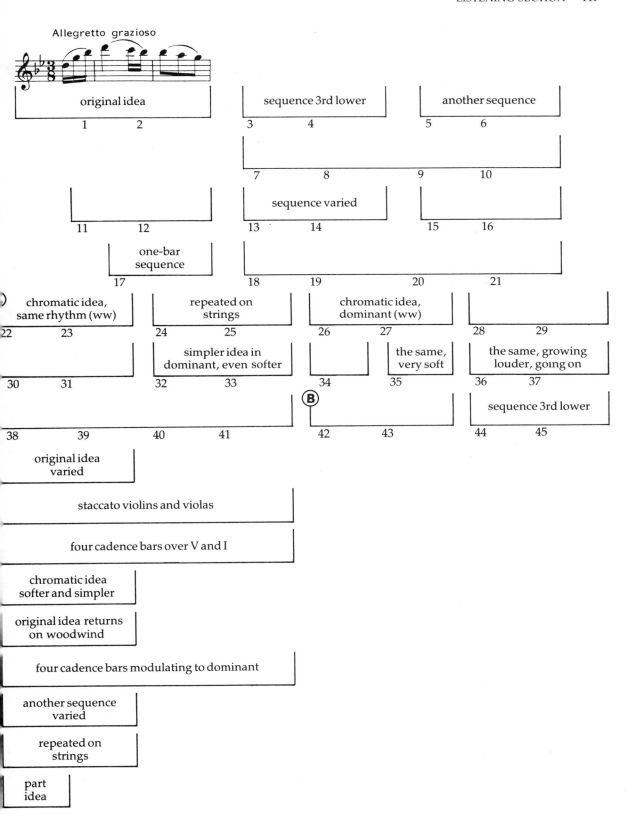

Listening test F

Read through the questions, then listen to the recording, which will b
played a number of times. Answer questions 1–7 on or near the
stave and questions 8–15 in the boxes at the foot of the page.

1   Add suitable phrase marks in the first four bars.
2   An accidental has been left out in bar 4; put it in.
3   Complete the notation where the violin has the tune for the first
    time.
4   Continue the violin part in bars 13–16.
5   Mark appropriately the point where the lower strings change their
    mode of playing and also the bar where they play normally again.
6   Mark with an x the bar where the music modulates to A minor.
7   Continue the melody in bars 24 and 25.

8   Which instrument has the tune at the beginning?
9   What do the accompanying strings do?
10 Which rhythmic figure occurs in bar 8?
11 What does the solo instrument play in bar 9: a scale, an arpeggio or
    a trill?
12 How does the melodic motive grow in bars 13–15?
13 The solo instrument is a transposing instrument and is pitched in A.
    Write out the first phrase as it would appear in the player's part.
14 Now listen to the remainder of the section. Mention two features as
    the music makes its way back to the tonic and the return of the first
    idea.
15 Mention two other points of interest which occur after the return.

Listening group G

1 Listen to the start of 'Autumn' from Vivaldi's *Four Seasons*. The peasants are celebrating in song and dance a good harvest. Notice the echoes every few bars.

The music here is printed without them. Copy it out, filling in the missing bars. Be careful to write them in the correct octave and listen for anywhere the echo is not quite exact. Mark the music with appropriate dynamics.

Say in what way the first two bars of the third line grow from the first bar of the piece.

2 Now listen to another movement from the *Four Seasons*. This extract is from the start of 'Spring'. As with 'Autumn', there are echoes which change from loud to soft. This movement suggests the song of birds and as so often with birds, there is some repetition and they sometimes sing in canon. An outline of the music is given for you to complete. It is written for a solo violin with two other violins. Listen carefully for the point where the first violin starts to imitate the solo violin in canon.

Solo and
Violin 1
p
4
f
7
tr
10
p
13
Solo
violin
tr
Violin 1
tr
Violin 2
solo
tr
tr
16
tr
tr
19
tr
tr

Listening test G

Look at the questions and then listen to the recording, which will be played a number of times. Answer questions 1–6 on or near the stave and questions 7–14 in the boxes at the foot of page.

This piece uses echoes and imitations in two ways. Loud phrases are answered by soft, and motives in the upper part are answered in the bass.

1   Add markings for loud and soft where appropriate.
2   Add trill signs where trills are played in the first line.
3   Complete the notation in bars 4–6.
4   Show bass imitations by writing the rhythm of the phrase in the correct places under the stave.
5   Complete the notation in bars 11 and 12.
6   This movement modulates to another key surprisingly early. The accidentals which would show this have been left out. Add them where necessary.

7   Name any bar in which there are chords of three or more parts.
8   Name any bar which has just a two-part texture.
9   Mention two ways in which the original idea is carried forward.
10   On which instrument is this piece performed?
11   A typical violin figure occurs in some bars. Which are these?
12   This extract is from the first part of a piece in binary form. When might it have been written?

Now listen to bars 20–32, which complete the first part.

13   List three features which occur in bars 20–23.
14   Comment briefly on the remaining bars.

Listening group H

1 Like many 18th-century suites, Handel's *Music for the Royal Fireworks* starts with a French overture. Handel uses two ideas to start the allegro in this movement: a two-bar fanfare for three trumpets and timpani answered by dotted rhythms on other instruments. Here is a framework for the first 27 bars. Copy it into your manuscript book. Then listen to the recording a number of times. Notice the way the fanfare and dotted rhythms overlap so that the sound is continuous.

Add the rhythm and tune to the first two fanfares at bars 1 and 5. Mark each other fanfare entry with a quaver rest in the correct bar. Then complete the framework with answers to the questions.

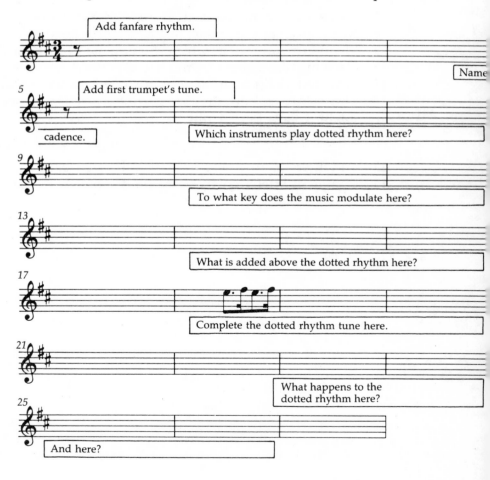

2 Here is the right-hand part of a March in D from one of the Anna Magdalena Bach notebooks. With its syncopated rhythm derived from the long note across the middle of the bar, it is a vigorous tune, and the bass part (in the left hand) complements the upper line and adds even more vitality to the music. Notice how the long note is stressed with a temporary clash with the bass part. Notice too the imitation of the interval of a 4th. The two hands are tuneful partners in two-part counterpoint.

Listen to the recording and then answer these questions.

a. Pairs of quavers are an important element in the upper part. In which bars do pairs of quavers come in the left hand?

b. Why do you think left-hand quavers come less often in the second section?

c. Where does the music modulate to the dominant?

d. Which key is that?

e. How would you describe bars 8 and 9 and 21 and 22?

f. What happens at bar 10?

g. What is the left hand playing under the sequence in bars 14 and 15?

h. This piece is in binary form. How do you know? Why do you think the second section is longer than the first?

3. Listen to the main tune from the 'March to the Scaffold' from Berlioz's *Symphonie fantastique*. It is strongly syncopated, both with long notes on off-beats and with stressed semiquavers in the dotted rhythms. Here is the melodic outline of the first four bars. Rewrite it with the rhythm and bar-lines added. The rhythms of the Handel and the Anna Magdalena Bach piece will help you.

Now listen again and answer these questions.

a. How many bars are added to the four-bar melody you have completed before it is repeated?
b. What happens after it is repeated?
c. Why do the instruments which play this music remind us of a military band?
d. Do the strings play anything in this extract? If so, what?

Now listen on further in the movement. Before the main tune returns again, there is an interlude which is full of surprises. Mention three of them. In what way is the music different when the tune comes back?

Listening test H

Look at the questions, then listen to the recording, which will be played a number of times. Answer questions 1–7 on or near the stave and questions 8–12 in the boxes at the foot of the sheet provided.

1 Complete the notation of the tune in bars 2 and 3.
2 Add notes and rests to complete bar 4.
3 Name the key in bar 8.
4 Continue the notation from bar 13 for six more beats. Name the musical device used.
5 There are more examples of this device before the end of the piece. Mark two of their appearances with square brackets above the stave.

6 The three-note idea marked X is used throughout the piece as a unifying motive. It appears in the bass in six places. Mark these, under the stave, with X.

7 Use Roman numerals to label the chords which form the cadence in bar 18.

8 Listen to the first three bars and comment on:
    a. the tune
    b. the texture
    c. the counterpoint.

9 Describe the way the idea in bar 5 grows in bars 6 and 7.

10 Name two instruments which play this music.

11 In what form is this piece? Give two reasons for your choice.

12 When might this piece have been written: about 1750, 1800, 1850 or 1900?

Listening group I

1 *Lilliburlero* and the opening of Mozart's A major Piano Sonata к331 have very similar rhythms and tunes. Here, the rhythms have become parted from their tunes and the music of both has been mixed up. Sort out the bits and pieces and reconstruct the first four bars of each tune.

The Mozart tune you sorted out in question 1 is part of the theme for a set of variations. Unusually, these form the first movement. Do you know any other sonatas or symphonies which start with a set of variations? Pieces with three or four movements are more likely to have a set of variations as their slow or last movements.

2   Here is another Mozart example in A major, the theme for a set of variations in the Clarinet Quintet. This time the variations, as is usual, make up the last movement. Notice its very simple form, which is given in outline.

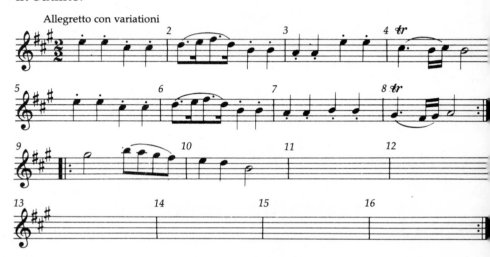

Allegretto con variationi

Listen to the recording several times and answer the questions below.

a. Which two instruments start the theme?
b. How would you describe the way they play in bars 1 and 2?
c. In which bar does the clarinet enter?
d. What cadence occurs in bar 4?
e. Where does the clarinet enter again?
f. What does the first violin play in bars 7 and 8?
g. What cadence completes the first section in bar 8?
h. Compare the music in the third line with that of the other lines.
i. How do bars 11 and 12 relate to bars 9 and 10?
j. Is the fourth line like the first or second line?
k. How does Mozart vary the texture of this 16-bar theme?
l. Is the piece in ternary or binary form? Give reasons for your answer.

Read through the following descriptions of the variations and coda. Then listen to the whole movement and list A–F in the order in which they occur in the piece.

A Bustling triplets accompany a tune on the violin which does not forget the dotted rhythm; some surprising *piano-forte* contrasts.

B A rush of continuous scales and broken-chord semiquavers, shared between clarinet and violin.

C The theme returns at a lively pace and hurries for home. Clarinet and cello almost seem to 'miss the boat'.

D A change of mode as the music darkens.

E A springy tune on the clarinet which is mostly above the theme.

F Slow and expressive with chromatic scales and arpeggio sweeps on the clarinet.

Listening test I

Read through the questions and then listen to the recording, which will be played a number of times. Answer questions 1–7 on or near the staves and questions 8–16 in the boxes at the foot of the answer sheet provided.

1 Complete the melody in bars 2, 4 and 6.
2 Add suitable dynamic marks under bars 5 and 6.
3 Add stems, tails and accidentals to bars 7 and 8.
4 At the point where the first idea returns, write a bass clef and notate three bars of the bass part in minims.
5 Add appropriate tempo markings above bar 16.
6 Add the violin melody in bars 16 and 17.
7 The note in bar 17 is held on and then joined to the next section. Add suitable marks to show this.

8 Comment on the rhythm of the first six bars.
9 Which instruments play the first six bars?
10 Which instrument has the tune from bar 7?
11 What else is important in bar 7?
12 Comment on the way the music is extended in bars 7–10.
13 Compare the lower strings in bars 1–3 with those in bars 11–13.
14 What is different in the treatment of the theme when it returns.
15 The last bar is an example of a traditional device used at the end of a piece in a minor key. What is it called?
16 In what form is this piece?

Listening test J

Stravinsky's *Histoire du soldat* tells the tale of a soldier who comes home on leave and sells his violin to the devil. The music is for a small ensemble consisting of a clarinet, cornet, trombone, percussion violin and double bass. The story is 'to be read, played and danced'

The story starts with the 'Soldier's March'. The double bass doggedly stomps along in duple time on its homeward trek. The other instruments jump in and out with their ideas and sometimes come together in agreement. The soldier throws off an odd motive or two on his violin. The music mostly marches in duple time with the double bass, but sometimes slips up by missing a quaver ($\frac{3}{8}$) or adding a beat ($\frac{3}{4}$).

Here are the main ideas. They are sometimes changed slightly when they come again in the piece and they are not always played by the same instruments.

A   double bass

almost all the time

B   cornet   clarinet

 later becomes

trombone   cornet

C   bassoon

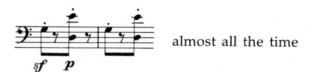

D   cornet

E   cornet

trombone

F   violin

G   bassoon

Listen to the music, an outline of which is printed on the test sheet. Complete it by putting appropriate letters in the circles where the main ideas are heard. In addition, write the names of the instruments where there are empty boxes. The rehearsal numbers are taken from the score.

Listening group K

1   As might be expected the Tartar's Dance from the *Polovtsian Dances* in Borodin's *Prince Igor* is strong, barbaric and powerful, like the warriors who perform it. It is also, like many dances, built up from four-bar phrases. Here are the melodic outlines of the different phrases; except for A, which is an introduction, they are all repeated a number of times. Listen to the recording and then list the order of the phrases in your notebook.

Now answer these questions about the music.

a. The introduction grows louder as the rhythm is repeated. Give four suitable dynamic marks to show this stepped crescendo.
b. What does 'sempre 8va' mean?
c. Comment on the harmony in phrase B. Of what is it an example?
d. Compare the accompaniment of phrase B with phrase C. Refer to harmony, rhythm and instrumentation.
e. How does the melody move down in phrase C?
f. What is different about the texture of phrase D?
g. In which key is it?
h. What happens to this phrase when it is repeated?
i. What is the new rhythmic figure in phrase D?

2 Another ferocious piece of Russian music is the 'Hut on Hen's Legs' from Mussorgsky's *Pictures at an Exhibition*. This is about the home of the witch Baba Yaga and depicts the hut 'taking off' into the air as its owner chases another victim.

Like a dance, the music is built of two- and four-bar phrases, but in the first eight bars, as the hut 'gets up steam', there are whole bars' rests, unexpected rhythms and very angular intervals. There is a lot of repetition. Follow the recording with the cues given. Then listen several times more so that you can answer the questions.

A What happens in these three bars?

+   3 bars

B What happens in these?

   +   3 bars

C How are the four extra bars changed?

   + 4 bars

D Which word do you think is written in these bars?

   × 4

E What happens each time these two bars are repeated? What does the left hand do? What is different about the texture?

   × 3 + D

F Where is the repeat slightly changed?

   × 2

G How is the tension raised in these bars?

   + 12 bars

H What happens to each repeat? How is the idea extended after the repeats?

I To which idea are these five phrases related?

J Is this idea related? If so, to what and how?

3 The incidental music Grieg wrote for Ibsen's play *Peer Gynt* is often heard on its own. The second movement in the first suite is called 'The Death of Åse' and comes from the scene where Peer's mother dies. Listen several times to the first eight bars and then complete the melody.

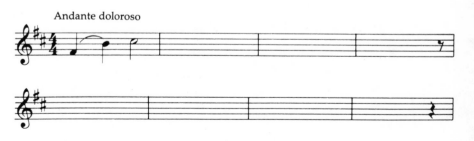

Mention two ways in which bars 1 and 2 differ from bars 5 and 6. This melody comes twice more. How is it different when it is played again?

After the second time, the music starts to sink down, with a repeated chromatic motive in the violins and a counterpoint in the violas.

Complete the viola line. Listen for a fragment of chromatic scale.
How many times is this four-bar phrase repeated?
What happens each time it is played again?
Describe the last few bars of the piece.

Listening test K

Read through the questions and then listen to the recording, which
will be played a number of times. Answer questions 1–7 on or near
the staves and questions 8–15 in the boxes at the foot of the test
sheet provided.

1 Complete bar 2, adding any articulation signs needed.
2 Continue the melody in bars 3 and 4.
3 An accidental has been omitted in bar 5; add it in the correct place.
4 Add suitable dynamic marks under bars 5–8.
5 Write in Roman numerals the chords used in bar 8.
6 Add the trombone part in bars 9–11, using the bass clef.
7 Add the tune in bars 13 and 14.

8 Which tempo marking is most suitable for this music: adagio molto,
   andante doloroso or allegro con brio?
9 Which families of instruments play in bars 1–8?
10 What is the musical device used in bars 3 and 4?
11 What rhythm is used on the last beat of bar 8?
12 Name two instruments which join in at bar 9.
13 How would you describe the music in bars 15 and 16: cheerful,
   menacing, pretty, playful or agitated?
14 How is this effect achieved?
15 This passage is taken from the overture to Wagner's *Flying Dutchman*.
   Do you think the first 14 bars of the extract are associated with the
   stormy sea, the mad Dutchman, the heroine or the sailors?

Background reference

Contents

Historical chart

Renaissance

Josquin Desprez	c1440-1521	Flemish
Tallis	c1505-1585	English
Palestrina	c1525-1594	Italian
Byrd	1543-1623	English
Giovanni Gabrieli	c1554-1612	Italian
Morley	c1557-1602	English
Dowland	1563-1626	English
Monteverdi	1567-1643	Italian
Weelkes	1576-1623	English

Baroque

Monteverdi	1567-1643	Italian
Schütz	1585-1672	German
Lully	1632-1687	French
Corelli	1653-1713	Italian
Purcell	1659-1695	English
Alessandro Scarlatti	1660-1725	Italian
François Couperin	1668-1733	French
Vivaldi	1678-1741	Italian
Rameau	1683-1764	French
J S Bach	1685-1750	German
Domenico Scarlatti	1685-1757	Italian
Handel	1685-1759	German
Boyce	1710-1779	English

Classical

C P E Bach	1714-1788	German
Gluck	1714-1787	German
Johann Stamitz	1717-1757	German
Haydn	1732-1809	Austrian
J C Bach	1735-1782	German
Mozart	1756-1791	Austrian
Beethoven	1770-1827	German
Rossini	1792-1868	Italian
Schubert	1797-1828	Austrian

1450
1500
1550
1600
1650
1700
1750
1800

notes

Renaissance

This period derives its name from the fact that it saw a rebirth of learning and in particular a revival of interest in and understanding of ancient Greek art and culture. Italian in origin, the movement gradually spread; its influence reached English music towards the end of the reign of Elizabeth I. It was a period of discovery and of a new realism. By the beginning of the 16th century, music was becoming very popular and both church and secular music flourished as they freed themselves from the more restrictive techniques of medieval music. Unaccompanied choral music was contrapuntal but was more closely related to the meaning of the words. Imitation between the voices unified the sound. Harmony became more important and expressive, with a more controlled use of dissonance than before. Instrument making of many kinds flourished and instrumental music assumed a more important role. Towards the end of the period, the first operas were written: these tried to link words even more closely with music by the use of recitative, in which a solo voice was accompanied by only a few simple chords.

Typical forms

Mass, motet (church music)
Madrigal, ballett, ayre (secular music)
Fantasia, division on a ground, various dance movements, often in pairs (instrumental music)

Fashionable instruments

Recorder, lute, viol (often used in collections of different sizes, called consorts), harpsichord (or 'virginals' in England)

Notable works

El grillo (The cricket)	Desprez
Missa Papae Marcelli	Palestrina
Sonata pian e forte alla quarta bassa	Giovanni Gabrieli
Mass in five parts	Byrd
Triumphs of Oriana (English madrigal collection)	
Fitzwilliam Virginal Book (collection of Elizabethan harpsichord pieces)	
Vespers of 1610	Monteverdi

aroque

The term 'Baroque' is borrowed from architecture and refers to the elaborate, sometimes dramatic decoration which aims for a grand effect. It is often emotional in its appeal. The start of the Baroque in music coincided with the birth of opera and oratorio. Early opera composers aimed to unite words and music in an expressive melodic line, simply accompanied. The accompaniment consisted of a bass line, on top of which chords were added. To make it easier to improvise the chords, the bass part was often 'figured'; this was known as figured bass or basso continuo (or 'continuous bass'). Basso continuo was the basis for most Baroque music. The harmonic framework provided the basis (even in solo works) on which expressive decoration was applied. The organ or harpsichord and bass string(s) usually formed the continuo and voices and other instruments wove their counterpoint over and around them. Normally a single mood or *Affekt* would dominate each movement, but beyond this dramatic effects were sought by contrasting different timbres, small and large groups, recitatives and arias and terraced dynamics. Instrumental music developed alongside vocal and both came together in opera and oratorio.

ypical forms

Opera, oratorio, cantata (vocal) (all make much use of recitative and the da capo aria)
Suites of dances, concerti grossi, Italian and French overtures, fugue, trio sonata (instrumental)

ashionable struments

Organ, harpsichord, violin (taking over from the less brilliant viol) and trumpet

otable works

L'Orfeo (1607) (first really successful opera)	Monteverdi
Dido and Aeneas (1689)	Purcell
The Four Seasons (c1725)	Vivaldi
Mass in B minor (assembled c1747–9)	J. S. Bach
The Well-tempered Clavier (1722–42)	J. S. Bach
Messiah (1742)	Handel
Keyboard sonatas (555 single movements)	Domenico Scarlatti

Classical

It is in this short period that much of the music we hear was composed. The era includes at least three giants of composition in Haydn, Mozart and Beethoven. As with all periods, its exact beginning and ending is a matter of opinion, but it has the hallmark of late 18th-century art. We associate Classical art and architecture with balance, purity of line and perfect control of form and medium. Much of the music from the Classical period can be said to have these qualities. It states its purpose clearly and it does not stay a moment too long. Within these well-judged proportions it expresses wide range of feelings without excess. The orchestra, which started to take shape in the later Baroque, lost its continuo and became the vehicle for many symphonies and concertos. The string quartet replaced the trio sonata as the favoured genre in chamber music and many sonatas were written for piano, either by itself or with another instrument. Instrumental music dominated, but Mozart wrote some of the finest operas of all time, illustrating the dramatic possibilities of Classical forms. Much of the music was simpler in line and harmony than that of the Baroque, and where it was contrapuntal (which was much less often) the counterpoint was less rugged. The most important structure was that of the sonata form, which embrace two subject areas opposed in key and often in mood. This is a principle difference between the Classical and Baroque approach and reflects in part a change in attitudes as people felt less inclined to accept without question every aspect of society.

Typical forms

Symphony, sonata, string quartet (these almost without exception included at least one movement in sonata form) (instrumental) Opera, mass (vocal) CONCERTO.

Fashionable instruments

Piano (which evolved during the period), clarinet (again, developed during the period), transverse flute (the flute as we know it, which replaced the recorder)

Notable works

Keyboard sonatas (over 200)	C. P. E. Bach
12 London Symphonies	Haydn
The Creation	Haydn
The Marriage of Figaro	Mozart
Piano concertos	Mozart
Symphony no.2	Beethoven
Early piano sonatas	Beethoven
String quartets op.18	Beethoven
The 'Trout' Quintet	Schubert
The Barber of Seville	Rossini

Romanticism

Beethoven	1770-1827	German
Weber	1786-1826	German
Schubert	1797-1828	Austrian
Berlioz	1803-1869	French
Mendelssohn	1809-1847	German
Chopin	1810-1849	Polish
Schumann	1810-1856	German
Liszt	1811-1886	Hungarian
Verdi	1813-1883	Italian
Wagner	1813-1886	German
Brahms	1833-1897	German
Tchaikovsky	1840-1893	Russian
Mahler	1860-1911	Austrian
Richard Strauss	1864-1949	German

Nationalism

Glinka	1804-1857	Russian
Smetana	1824-1884	Bohemian
Borodin	1833-1887	Russian
Mussorgsky	1839-1881	Russian
Grieg	1843-1907	Norwegian
Rimsky-Korsakov	1844-1908	Russian
Albéniz	1860-1911	Spanish
Falla	1876-1946	Spanish
Kodály	1881-1967	Hungarian

00

25

50

75

00

25

Romanticism

Romanticism in art, literature and music moved away from Classicism by allowing emotional content to dominate form. In contrast to Classical music, Romantic music can be said to express its feelings openly and freely, though occasionally it becomes over-indulgent in the process. Romanticism spans the 19th century and was at its most intense in the middle of the century. Music and literature were closely associated and throughout the period opera was a telling force. The two arts were also linked in song cycles and programme music. Nature, myth, magic, death, ghosts, far-away places and olden days, as well as love with its joys and agonies, were all subjects which inspired composers directly or indirectly through stories, poetry and painting.

Early Romanticism was largely German and the music of Weber and Schubert extended the Classical idiom. As the period progressed the music became richer in texture and ranged wider in harmony. Melodies became more song-like. The orchestra expanded and the piano became more powerful. Virtuoso performers like Liszt and Paganini were greatly admired and composers like Wagner and Mahler were fine conductors.

Typical forms

Opera (Verdi), music drama (Wagner)
Programme music (concert overtures, tone poems and symphonies with stories or voices)
Song cycles
Short piano pieces (often in collections of several numbers)

Fashionable instruments

Full orchestra, concert grand piano, violin (as a virtuoso instrument), cor anglais

Notable works

Der Freischütz (The marksman) (1821)	Weber
William Tell (1829)	Rossini
The Flying Dutchman (1841)	Wagner
Rigoletto (1851)	Verdi
Tristan und Isolde (1859)	Wagner
Aida (1870)	Verdi
Die schöne Müllerin (The maid of the mill) (song cycle) (1823)	Schubert
Symphonie fantastique (1831)	Berlioz
Carnaval (piano suite) (1835)	Schumann
Violin Concerto in E minor (1844)	Mendelssohn
Four ballades and other piano music	Chopin
Piano Concerto in A minor (1845)	Schumann
Swan Lake (full-scale ballet) (1876)	Tchaikovsky
Symphony no.6 ('Pathétique') (1893)	Tchaikovsky

Till Eulenspiegel (tone poem) (1895)	Richard Strauss
Symphony no.4 (1900)	Mahler
Das Lied von der Erde (The song of the earth) (1909)	Mahler

Nationalism

Nationalism was one aspect of the Romantic movement. In Germany, it was almost indistinguishable from Romanticism in general, since at the beginning of the 19th century Germany dominated the musical scene. But by the middle of the century, pride in national culture and heritage was growing and composers from other countries tried to break the bond of German influence. Russia and Bohemia at this time, and Norway a little later, were the countries most prominent in the movement. In Russia composers like Glinka and Mussorgsky based operas on national stories and adopted some typical non-German techniques like repetition (sometimes with variation) in place of thematic development. In Bohemia (now part of Czechoslovakia), Smetana wrote music about his country, and he and Dvořák used Slovak rhythms and melodic features in their music. Grieg in Norway also embodied folksong elements into his idiom.

As the 19th century moved into the 20th, composers from other countries like Spain, Hungary and Great Britain began to shake off German domination and to draw new vigour from their folk heritage.

Typical forms

Opera, choral music
Tone poems and other symphonic music with national associations
Suites of national and folk dances

Fashionable instruments

Full orchestra and, later, instruments such as the Hungarian cimbalom which add a national flavour

Notable works

Ruslan and Lyudmila (1842)	Glinka
Prince Igor (completed by Rimsky-Korsakov and Glazunov after Borodin's death)	Borodin
The Bartered Bride (1864)	Smetana
Boris Godunov (1869)	Mussorgsky
Má vlast (My country) (six tone poems)	Smetana
Slavonic dances (1878–86)	Dvořák
Norwegian dances	Grieg
Peer Gynt (incidental music) (1876)	Grieg
Iberia (12 piano pieces) (1906–9)	Albéniz
Psalmus Hungaricus (1923)	Kodály

20th-century music

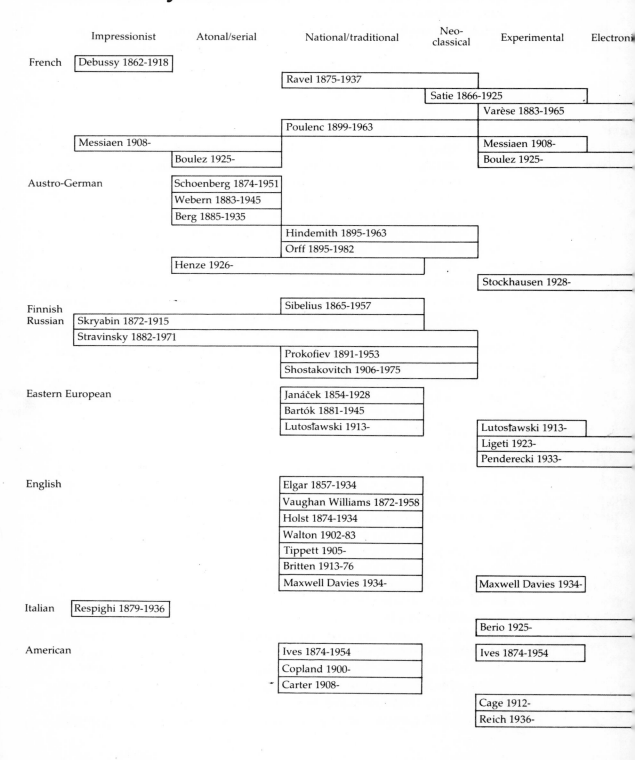

	Impressionist	Atonal/serial	National/traditional	Neo-classical	Experimental	Electronic
French	Debussy 1862-1918					
			Ravel 1875-1937			
				Satie 1866-1925		
					Varèse 1883-1965	
			Poulenc 1899-1963			
	Messiaen 1908-				Messiaen 1908-	
		Boulez 1925-			Boulez 1925-	
Austro-German		Schoenberg 1874-1951				
		Webern 1883-1945				
		Berg 1885-1935				
			Hindemith 1895-1963			
			Orff 1895-1982			
		Henze 1926-				
					Stockhausen 1928-	
Finnish			Sibelius 1865-1957			
Russian	Skryabin 1872-1915					
	Stravinsky 1882-1971					
			Prokofiev 1891-1953			
			Shostakovitch 1906-1975			
Eastern European			Janáček 1854-1928			
			Bartók 1881-1945			
			Lutosławski 1913-		Lutosławski 1913-	
					Ligeti 1923-	
					Penderecki 1933-	
English			Elgar 1857-1934			
			Vaughan Williams 1872-1958			
			Holst 1874-1934			
			Walton 1902-83			
			Tippett 1905-			
			Britten 1913-76			
			Maxwell Davies 1934-		Maxwell Davies 1934-	
Italian	Respighi 1879-1936					
					Berio 1925-	
American			Ives 1874-1954		Ives 1874-1954	
			Copland 1900-			
			Carter 1908-			
					Cage 1912-	
					Reich 1936-	

npressionist
1880–c1920)

Mostly French. Linked with French painters and poets, it stresses the direct effect of light, mood and emotions. Music often given titles, although Debussy, in the preludes, places these after the music. Techniques used include the use of chords for their own special effect, rather than as part of a progression, parallel 7ths and 9ths, whole-tone and other exotic scales, chromaticism and a sensitive, evocative use of orchestral colour. It is a misunderstanding to think that Impressionism, either in art or music, is vague and unstructured; it is often, as is so much French art, concise and precise.

tonal/serial
1910–c1960)

Mostly associated with Austria and Germany. Much of the music is concerned with the inner workings of the mind as revealed by Freud. There is also a strong link with the Expressionist painters. Techniques at first grew out of late Romantic chromaticism, which increasingly broke down the feeling for a tonal centre. Often frenzied, dissonant, intense and emotional. In the 1920s, atonal music was systematised into 12-note serialism, in which the order of the 12 notes was established for each piece. This period was dominated by Schoenberg and his pupils Berg and Webern, sometimes called the Second Viennese School; their influence was gradually felt in much mid-century music. Webern, with his spare textures and miniature forms, was a particular influence. In the 1950s, the ordering of pitch was extended to cover rhythm and metre and dynamics and timbre, in total serialism. This very mathematical approach had but a short fashion, and as if by reaction gave way to very free, experimental chance music.

ational/
aditional

Represents a broad band of composers from many countries, many of whom, like Bartók and Vaughan Williams, had strong national roots in their idiom. Techniques are largely traditional in origin, but have been dragged forward to meet the needs of 20th-century ideas and anxieties. A number of composers have been influenced by jazz. Much fine, sincere music has been written.

eo-classical
1920–c1950)

Trend which reacted against the excesses of late Romantic chromaticism and orchestration. The movement started, partly as an economy measure, after the First World War. Stravinsky is the key figure, but many other composers wrote some neo-classical music. Often characterised by simple melodies which suddenly switch direction into unexpected keys and by direct harmonies spiced with wrong notes. Dissonance is more playful than intense, and instrumental combinations and forms are inspired by those of the

Baroque and Classical styles. Except for German neo-classicism, which is often serious in intent, much of the music is light-hearted and witty, although some moving works, for instance Stravinsky's *Symphony of Psalms*, can be said to be neo-classical.

Experimental (before and after 1950)

A broad term to cover a wide range of music composed in the last hundred years, starting with Ives and his experiments setting different keys, rhythms and instrumental groupings against each other. Other techniques employed use prepared instruments (Cage), modified methods of playing and singing (Berio), chance selection of material and open form (Stockhausen), indeterminacy (Penderecki), total serialism (Messiaen), graphic and text scores (Cage), textural densities and note clusters (Ligeti), microtones (Partch) and spatial experiments with the placing of sound sources. Sometimes known as the music of the avant garde (following the latest trends).

Electronic (1940 onwards)

Dependent on the invention of the tape recorder, most early experiments were in the form of 'musique concrète'. This meant that the sounds used were from real life, but that their presentation was modified with a tape recorder or electronically in some other way. Pure electronic music followed with the sounds being produced by electronic generators of one type or another. Many composers now combine live performers with tape, the two sound sources interacting with each other.

Structure and form

A   B   A

Each of the three sections is usually complete in itself and section A ends in the home key or tonic. The second section might be in a contrasting key, for instance the dominant or the relative minor. A short coda is sometimes added.

Popular in the 17th century when the return of A would be embellished with additional ornamentation. Many operatic arias are in ternary form.

rondo form

A   B   A   C   A

An extension of ternary form in which there are two episodes in contrasting keys. Section A is always in the tonic and might have slight decorative treatment on its return. The structure may be extended with a further episode. A coda might be added at the end.

Popular since early times, a simple way of extending a movement.

binary form

A:‖:B:‖

Usually a single-mood form with little contrast other than of key. The first section either ends on the dominant with an imperfect cadence in the home key, or in the dominant, having modulated. The second section moves from the dominant, sometimes by way of a number of other keys, back to the tonic. For this reason, the second section might be somewhat longer. Both sections are repeated.

Extensively used for short dances and other movements in the Baroque period, when its single mood was favoured. Little used since.

sonata form

A   B:‖ Development   A   B

An extension of binary form in which contrasting subject matter is introduced in the dominant (or less often some other key) within the first section (or exposition), which ends in the dominant. The second section (as in binary form) starts in the dominant, moves through a number of keys in a development and then leads back to the tonic. This coincides with the recapitulation (or return) of the first subject, the contrasting second subject following, now in the tonic key. A coda is often added.

Exposition :‖ Development   Recapitulation

As with binary form, both sections were at first repeated. Later the repeat was confined to the exposition, which was balanced by the development and recapitulation.

The major structural principle for the second part of the 18th century. Most sonatas and symphonies have an opening movement in sonata form, which for this reason is sometimes called first-movement form.

Rondo-sonata or sonata-rondo form

A B A C A B A

A mixture, as its name implies, of two forms. It takes its pattern from rondo form and its key structure from sonata form. The first episode (B) is usually announced in the dominant, but returns towards the end in the tonic. The second subject in sonata form is treated in the same way. The second episode (C) may include some development of material. It is often in a minor key. A coda might be added.

A favourite structure for last movements in the Classical period.

Variation form

A A^1 A^2 A^3 $\rightarrow$

A theme is announced and then presented several times in varied ways. The theme is usually straightforward so that its basic structure is easily recognisable. Variation may be rhythmic, melodic, figurative and sometimes harmonic. Texture and timbre may also be varied. Early sets of variations remained in the same key, except for an excursion into the minor (or into the major, if the theme was minor). Later sets sometimes ranged further afield.

Popular from the 16th century onwards, when the form was often known as divisions on a ground, the ground being the bass line and perhaps its harmony. Later, variation form was either used independently, as in a theme and variations, or as a movement in a sonata or symphony, in particular the slow or last movement.

rger forms

te

A set of dance movements usually all in the same key and sometimes sharing common melodic motives. Very popular in the Baroque period, when the four basic dances were the allemande (a German dance in quadruple time with a short upbeat), the courante (a running dance from France), the sarabande (a somewhat stately dance in triple time with a stressed second beat, from Latin America and Spain) and the gigue (a fast, lively dance in compound time, from the British Isles).

To these basic dances, others were added according to fashion, the most popular being the minuet (a French dance in a graceful triple time). Sometimes a piece for a smaller group of players was sandwiched between the minuet and its repeat. It became known as a trio, because it was often for just three instruments.

Besides the dance suite, in the 19th and 20th centuries many orchestral suites have been compiled from music originally written for the theatre or cinema.

nata

Originally just an instrumental piece which was 'sounded', in contrast to a vocal piece, or cantata, which was sung. The form gradually evolved until by the middle to late 18th century the sonata (along with its orchestral cousin, the symphony) had become the most important form.

Sonatas usually have three or four movements in the following plan:

First movement: sonata form (sometimes the weightiest movement)
Second movement: generally a slow movement in a simpler form
Third movement: a minuet (or scherzo) with trio
Fourth movement: a rondo-sonata or sometimes a set of variations

Sonatas were written for solo piano, various duos and other chamber-music combinations, including the string quartet; when for the last combination, they were called 'string quartets' instead of sonatas.

mphony

The orchestral relation of the sonata. Originally a symphony – the word derives from the Greek *syn* ('together') and *phōnē* ('sounding') – was an instrumental movement introducing an opera, cantata or suite. Like the sonata, it gradually evolved to its dominating position in the Classical period. Most classical symphonies have four movements and a good number have a slow introduction to the first movement. During the Romantic period, the symphony continued to evolve. It grew longer and, following the example of Beethoven's

Ninth Symphony, voices were sometimes added. At the same time, the slow movement was often placed third, which allowed a lively scherzo to contrast directly with a perhaps more extensive and reflective first movement.

Concerto

There are three broad types of concerto.

The concerto grosso is a Baroque form in which a small group of soloists (the concertino) interacted with a larger body (the ripieno), with which it often shared material. The instrumental combinations varied considerably. There was little brilliant display, the vitality of the music arising from the interplay of the groups. Bach's Brandenburg Concertos are fine examples of concerti grossi.

The solo concerto is usually much more brilliant, with the soloist pitted against the orchestra in a display of virtuosity. The excitement arises from the soloist alternately pleading and wrestling with the more powerful opposing forces. Solo concertos first gained popularity in the late Baroque, grew immensely in stature with Mozart's piano concertos, and have flourished ever since.

During the 20th century a number of important concertos for orchestra have been written. These resemble symphonies, but tend to allow more highlighting of individual instruments and groups in the course of the music. Famous examples have been written by Bartók, Tippett and Lutosławski.

Overture

A single-movement form traditionally used as an introduction to an opera or oratorio. It developed during the 17th century in two ways. The French overture (originated by Lully) had two or three sections: the first was slow, with considerable use of dotted rhythms; the second section was lively and contrapuntal, with imitative entries; where there was a third section, this either recalled briefly the opening or was a dance movement.

The Italian overture had three sections, quick–slow–quick. It was also known as the 'sinfonia' and unlike the French overture was not contrapuntal. It was the basis of the Classical symphony.

By the Classical period, the French overture had dropped out of fashion and most overtures were little different from the first movement of a symphony. They were frequently detached from their role and used as an introduction to a concert. During the 19th century, the quite independent concert overture became popular. Curiously, in the same period, the shorter prelude was used to introduce many operas.

Typical ensembles

16th–17th centuries	Consort	A group of similar instruments of different pitches roughly equivalent in range to voices, e.g. a consort of viols or recorders. Also a mixed ensemble, as in Morley's *Consort Lessons* (1599 and 1611), of treble viol or violin, flute or recorder, bass viol, lute, cittern and bandora; the term 'broken consort' is sometimes used for such a mix.
17th–18th centuries	Trio sonata	Two violins (or oboes, recorders or flutes etc), harpsichord, cello or bass viol; the term trio refers to the fact that the duo partners are accompanied by a third, continuo line, shared between keyboard and bass instrument.
18th–19th centuries	String quartet	Two violins, viola and cello (no double bass)
	String trio	Violin, viola and cello
	String quintet	String quartet plus viola or cello
	Clarinet quintet	String quartet plus clarinet
	Piano trio	Piano, violin and cello (not three pianos!)
	Wind quartet	Flute, oboe, clarinet and bassoon (in a wind octet, each instrument is doubled)
19th century	Wind quintet	Flute, oboe, clarinet, horn and bassoon
	Septet	Variable: Beethoven's op.20 for example has violin, viola, horn, clarinet, bassoon, cello and bass
	String octet	Variable: Mendelssohn's op.20 has four violins, two violas and two cellos

Octet	Variable: Schubert's has string quartet plus double bass, clarinet, horn and bassoon
Piano quintet	Piano plus string quartet; but Schubert's 'Trout' Quintet has piano, violin, viola, cello and double bass
20th century	Many mixed ensembles of varying combinations. Typical examples are:

Ravel: Introduction and Allegro (1906), harp, string quartet, flute and clarinet.

Stravinsky: Octet (1923), flute, clarinet, two bassoons, two trumpets, tenor trombone and tuba

Bartók: Contrasts (1938), violin, clarinet and piano

Messiaen: Quatuor pour la fin du temps (Quartet for the end of time) (1940), violin, clarinet, cello and piano

Boulez: Le marteau sans maître (The hammer without a master) (1955) flute, viola, guitar, vibraphone, percussion and voice.

Short glossary

Aria

An extended solo vocal piece, usually associated with opera and oratorio. In the 18th century nearly always in A B A form. Often introduced with a recitative. By the 19th century the aria had become more elaborate and flexible in form.

Atonal

Music without a tonal centre or keynote. At the end of the 19th century, some music became so chromatic that the tonal centre was lost. Early in the 20th century this instability was exploited for expressive purposes.

Cadenza

Originally an improvised flourish on the final cadence of an aria or solo instrumental piece. A chance for the soloist to 'show off' technical skills, it ended with a trill to signal that the accompaniment should rejoin. Later elaborated into a longer passage usually towards the end of a concerto movement. By the 19th century, few cadenzas were improvised.

anon A contrapuntal piece in which one or more voices or parts strictly imitate each other at a fixed distance. The imitation could be at the same pitch, or at the octave, or at any other interval. Some more complex canons use other devices like augmentation, diminution or playing backwards. A round is a form of canon which revolves round and round until the performers decide to stop.

oda An additional section added after what might have been the final cadence of a movement. In its simplest form, no more than a couple of chords, in its extended form (as so often with Beethoven) a substantial balancing section, often with further development of material.

Contrapuntal The adjective describing a piece which uses counterpoint.

Da capo Literally, 'from the head', as in the head or source of a river. In music, it means go back to the beginning and is abbreviated D.C. Arias in A B A form are often called da capo arias because they go back to the beginning after the second section.

Divertimento A suite of music of a light-hearted nature which would make a diversion at an entertainment or meal. Always for a small group of players. Mozart wrote 25 divertimenti for one combination or another. Alternative names are serenade or cassation.

ugue A contrapuntal piece in which a number of parts (or voices, as they are called) take flight in turn. Each voice enters in turn with an idea called the subject. The second voice has the subject in the dominant (this is called the 'answer'), while the first voice may have a countersubject. When all the voices have entered, the exposition is complete and the music flows into a middle section. This alternates a number of subject-and-answer entries with episodes, which are usually derived from the same ideas. The middle section modulates through a number of keys before moving into the final section, which may raise the tension with a stretto where the voices squash in on each other with closer entries. Fugue is a disciplined procedure in a very flexible structure: no two fugues are exactly alike in form.

A fugato is a fugue-like passage, often occurring in an otherwise non-contrapuntal piece.

Glissando A slide across the sounds between two pitches. On a piano all the white notes, or all the black notes. On a harp, where it is a much used effect, a slide across all the strings as they are set at the time. On a trombone, string instrument or pedal timpani, a real glissando which does not distinguish the intervening pitches is possible. A

	portamento on a string instrument is a very light type of glissando, carrying the sound of one note towards the next.
Homophonic	A style in which a number of parts or voices move together, with little or no rhythmic independence, as in most hymn tunes. Opposite of polyphonic.
Interlude	A piece played between scenes or acts in a play or opera.
Intermezzo	Originally a light entertainment between more serious music, but by the 19th century the term was used as an alternative to interlude. As with the prelude, Romantic composers used the word as a title for short piano pieces.
Leitmotif	A leading motive or short phrase which is associated with a person, thing or idea in a piece of programme music or an opera. It often undergoes a transformation during the piece. Wagner did not invent the idea, but he developed it to its highest form.
Lied (plural lieder)	German song (or songs) from about the time of Schubert onwards. Lieder may be either in simple verse form (strophic) or be through-composed in an extended form. Whether a song is lyrical or dramatic, the accompaniment, usually for piano, is of great importance in setting the mood.
Madrigal	A composition for a number of singers, usually but not always without accompaniment. It dates from 13th-century Italy, but in this country is usually associated with such Elizabethan composers as Byrd, Morley and Weelkes. Texts were often pastoral or amorous.
Motet	A sacred unaccompanied vocal piece, similar in period and style to the madrigal.
Polyphonic	A style in which parts or voices combine together while at the same time keeping their independence of rhythm and line. The opposite of homophonic. Madrigals and motets were mostly polyphonic.
Postlude	A piece played at the end, e.g. a piano solo at the end of a song cycle as in Schumann's *Dichterliebe*.
Prelude	A piece played before a fugue or passacaglia, for instance, or as an introduction to a suite, song cycle or opera. Chopin and Debussy detached the prelude from its introductory function and wrote sets of self-contained short pieces called preludes.
Recitative	A passage sung in free speech-rhythm telling the story in an opera or oratorio. Often introduces an aria. When simply accompanied by continuo it is known as recitative *secco* (dry recitative); when more fully and expressively accompanied it is called recitative *accompagnato* (accompanied recitative).

scherzo	Literally a 'joke'. Beethoven, in his symphonies and some sonatas, replaced the more stately minuet and trio with a lively, high-spirited scherzo and trio. Again, as with the prelude and intermezzo, in the 19th century the scherzo became a self-contained piano piece.
serialism	A system of organising the 12 notes of the chromatic scale in a series or note-row, which formed the basis of a movement or composition. The original order of notes could be inverted, played backwards (retrograde), or played backwards in its inverted form (retrograde inversion). Strictly, no note would reappear until the remaining 11 notes had been heard, but in practice this is not always observed, especially as the notes can appear at the same time, as chords. Schoenberg evolved the system in the 1920s as a rationalisation of atonalism.
tierce de Picardie (Picardy 3rd)	A name given to a major 3rd used in the final chord of a piece or section in the minor.
toccata	A delicate, rapid 'touch' piece sometimes used in place of a prelude, especially before a fugue. Later often the final movement in a suite or symphony, e.g. Widor's Fifth Symphony for organ.
tonality	The key of a piece. A pull towards a particular tonic or home sound. Up to the 20th century all music was tonal. In the 20th century, besides atonal music, which has no clear key, there have been pieces and passages written in two keys (bitonal) and in many keys at the same time (polytonal).

Transposing instruments

Some orchestral instruments, and in a brass band all but the bass trombone, are transposing instruments. This means that their parts are written at one pitch but sound at another, called 'concert pitch'. The reasons for treating them in this way are historical and practical. The notation for horns and trumpets dates back to the time before the invention of valves and pistons, when extra crooks (or coils of tubing) were inserted into the instrument in order to increase the length of tube. Clarinets are made in different sizes, but are notated in a way that allows the same fingerings to be used for each instrument. This is not like the descant and treble recorders, which use different fingerings to produce the same note. Brass band instruments (except the bass trombone) are all traditionally written in the treble clef to simplify reading when switching from one instrument to another. They transpose as much as two octaves and a note lower than their written pitch. Saxophones, which are often played by clarinettists, transpose in a similar way.

To write for a transposing instrument, always relate the sound to the note C. Whenever the note C is written, the 'name of the instrument' will sound: for instance, a clarinet in B flat will sound a written C as B flat and a horn in F will sound it as F. Then all that has to be remembered is whether the instrument is one of the very few which sound higher than the note which is written, like the trumpet in F and the cornet in E flat.

When using a key signature, take the interval of transposition (a tone for a clarinet in B flat) and write for the instrument in the key which is that interval above the sounding key like this:

sounding key   written for clarinet in B flat

When writing without a key signature, as with horns, decide on the interval of transposition (e.g. a perfect 5th for a horn in F) and write exactly at that interval above the sound like this:

sounding notes   written for horn in F

Be sure to add any necessary accidentals to keep the interval correct.

Study the tables of transposing instruments on the following pages

Table 1 shows the sound produced when written middle C is played on a transposing instrument (use this table when conducting or listening).

Table 2 shows the note to write to produce the sound middle C on a transposing instrument (use this table when composing or arranging).

Transposing instruments:
Table 1
showing the sound produced
when middle C is written
(conductors and listeners use
this table)

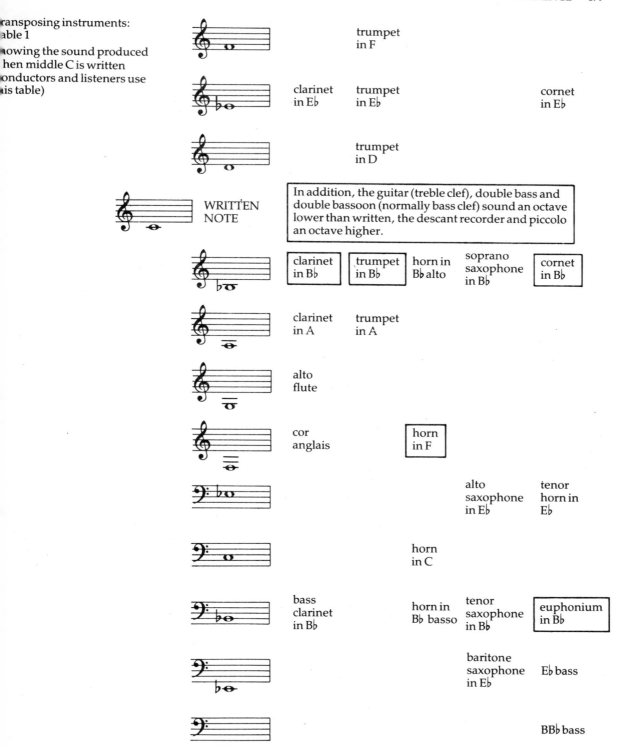

trumpet
in F

clarinet   trumpet   cornet
in Eb   in Eb   in Eb

trumpet
in D

WRITTEN
NOTE

In addition, the guitar (treble clef), double bass and
double bassoon (normally bass clef) sound an octave
lower than written, the descant recorder and piccolo
an octave higher.

clarinet   trumpet   horn in   soprano   cornet
in Bb   in Bb   Bb alto   saxophone   in Bb
                               in Bb

clarinet   trumpet
in A   in A

alto
flute

cor   horn
anglais   in F

                                alto   tenor
                                saxophone   horn in
                                in Eb   Eb

                      horn
                      in C

bass   horn in   tenor   euphonium
clarinet   Bb basso saxophone   in Bb
in Bb   in Bb

                                baritone
                                saxophone   Eb bass
                                in Eb

                                            BBb bass

Transposing instruments
Table 2

showing the notes to write to produce
the sound middle C
(use this table when composing
or arranging)

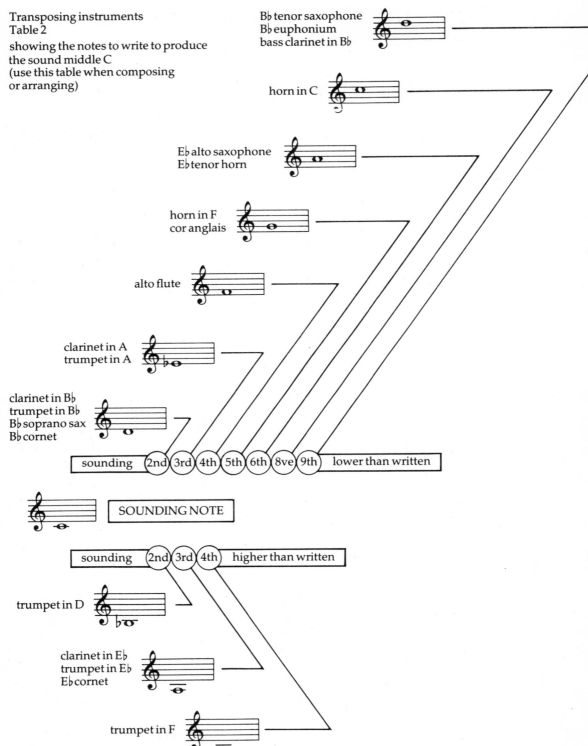

Orchestral instruments and their ranges

oodwind

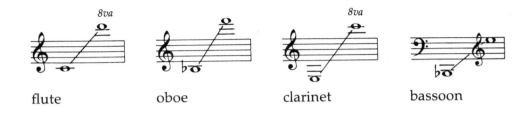

flute   oboe   clarinet   bassoon

rass

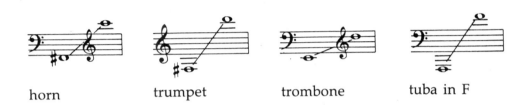

horn   trumpet   trombone   tuba in F

ercussion

tched

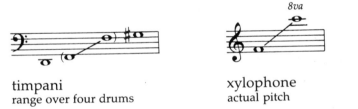

timpani
range over four drums

xylophone
actual pitch

glockenspiel
two 8ves higher

definite pitch   snare drum   bass drum   tambourine   cymbals

trings

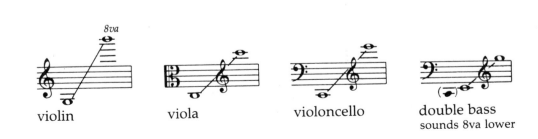

violin   viola   violoncello   double bass
sounds 8va lower

Orchestral evolution

Bach Suite in D BWV1068 c1730	Haydn 'Surprise' Symphony 1791	Beethoven Ninth Symphony 1823	Stravinsky Rite of Spring 1913
		piccolo	2 piccolos
	2 flutes	2 flutes	2 flutes
			alto flute
3 oboes	2 oboes	2 oboes	4 oboes
			cor anglais
			Eb clarinet
	2 clarinets	2 clarinets	3 clarinets
			2 bass clarinets
1 bassoon	2 bassoons	2 bassoons	3 bassoons
		contra bassoon	contra bassoon
	2 horns	4 horns	8 horns
			trumpet in D
3 trumpets	2 trumpets	2 trumpets	4 trumpets
		3 trombones	3 trombones
			2 tubas
			small timpani
2 timpani	2 timpani	2 timpani	4 timpani (2 players)
		bass drum	bass drum
		cymbals	cymbals
		triangle	triangle
			tambourine
			gong
			antique cymbals
			güiro
strings	strings	strings	strings
continuo			

Band instrumentation

Jazz band (Duke Ellington) 1940	Brass band	British military band	American concert or wind band
		1 piccolo	2 piccolos
		1 flute	2 flutes
		1 oboe	2 oboes
		E♭ clarinet	E♭ clarinet
clarinet		14 clarinets	3 clarinets
			alto clarinet
		2 bass clarinets	bass clarinet
		2 bassoons	2 bassoons
2 alto saxophones		alto saxophone	2 alto saxophones
tenor saxophone		tenor saxophone	tenor saxophone
baritone saxophone			baritone saxophone
	E♭ cornet		
	10 cornets	4 cornets	3 cornets
	flugelhorn		
	3 E♭ horns		4 E♭ horns
	2 baritones	2 baritones	baritone
	2 euphoniums	2 euphoniums	euphonium
		4 bombardons	
	2 E♭ basses		
	2 BB♭ basses		
3 trumpets		2 trumpets	2 trumpets
		4 horns in F	4 horns in F
3 trombones	3 trombones	3 trombones	3 trombones
			tubas
percussion	percussion	percussion	percussion
piano			
guitar			
string bass		string bass (when not marching)	string bass (optional)

Some Italian performance terms

Speed or tempo

adagio	slow, at ease
allegro	quickly, lightly and brightly
andante	going on, not too fast and not too slow
largo	broad and slow
lento	slow
moderato	at a moderate pace
presto	quick
vivace	lively

Change of tempo

accelerando	gradually quicker
allargando	broadening, getting slower
rallentando	running down, getting slower
ritenuto	held back, putting the brake on
stringendo	drawing together, getting quicker and quicker

Qualifying terms

con	with, as in *con spirito*, with spirit
ma	but, as in *piano ma sonoroso*, soft but sonorous
meno	less, as in *meno mosso*, less movement, slower
più	more, as in *più forte*, louder (often used between *f* and *ff*).
non troppo	not too much, as in *allegro non troppo*, not too quickly
molto	much, as in *molto crescendo*, a big increase in sound

Terms for mood and manner

agitato	agitated
dolce	sweetly
furioso	furiously
giocoso	humorously
grazioso	gracefully
legato	smoothly, joined up
leggiero	lightly
maestoso	majestically
marcato	marked (*ben marcato*, well marked)
mesto	sadly
tranquillo	tranquil

Force and intensity

pianissimo	*pp*	very soft
piano	*p*	soft
mezzo-piano	*mp*	moderately soft
mezzo-forte	*mf*	moderately loud
forte	*f*	loud
fortissimo	*ff*	very loud
crescendo	*cresc.*	get louder (gradually)
diminuendo	*dim.*	get softer (gradually)
sforzando	*sf*	reinforce (accent)
morendo		dying away
perdendosi		losing itself

Rudiment review

Contents

1 Pitch and notation

The word pitch refers to the height or depth of a sound. High sounds are produced when a string or a column of air vibrates quickly, low sounds when they vibrate slowly. The speed of vibration is known as the frequency. The note A that is used for tuning has a frequency of 440 vibrations per second.

The stave

Relative pitch is notated on a five-line stave.

Notes are written on a line

or in a space.

The higher the note, the higher the sound.

                                      lower   higher

The musical alphabet has seven letters – A, B, C, D, E, F and G – which are repeated for higher or lower notes as necessary.

Before the exact pitch of a note can be shown, one line of the stave must be fixed at a certain pitch. This is done by means of a clef.

Clefs

The treble or G clef   The bass or F clef

is wrapped round the second line up and fixes it as G above middle C.

is wrapped round the fourth line up and fixes it as F below middle C. The two dots enclose the same line.

In addition to the treble and bass clefs, some instruments, such as the viola and tenor trombone, play from music written in a C clef. This is because the sounds they make occupy a middle range between the G and F clefs.
Unlike the G and F clefs, the C clef has several positions. (The other clefs were similarly moveable in earlier times.) According to its position on the stave, the C clef changes its name.

When it fixes the middle line as middle C it is called an

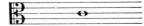

alto clef and is used by the viola.

When it fixes the fourth line up as middle C, it is called a

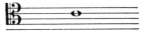

tenor clef and is used by the tenor trombone and by the cello and bassoon in their higher ranges.

ch names

Once the name of a line is fixed with a clef, the other notes fall into place. When written alphabetically, they alternate line–space–line–space and so on.

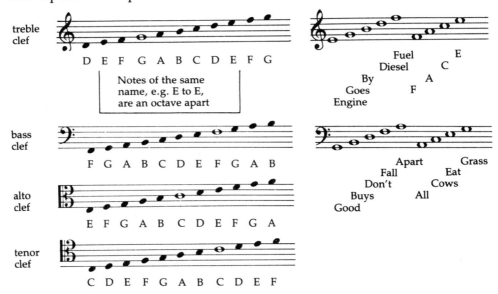

treble clef

D E F G A B C D E F G

Notes of the same name, e.g. E to E, are an octave apart

Fuel
Diesel
By
Goes
Engine
F
A
C
E

bass clef

F G A B C D E F G A B

Apart   Grass
Fall   Eat
Don't   Cows
Buys   All
Good

alto clef

E F G A B C D E F G A

tenor clef

C D E F G A B C D E F

ger lines

Pitches higher or lower than those that can be written on the stave are written with the help of leger lines, above or below it. These follow on from the pattern established by the clef in use.

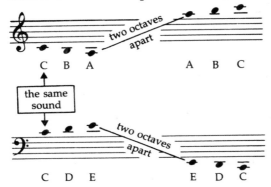

two octaves apart

C B A   A B C

the same sound

two octaves apart

C D E   E D C

The brace

Where an instrument, for instance the piano or harp, has a large range and is normally played with two hands, a pair of staves are joined together with a brace. Clefs are added as needed.

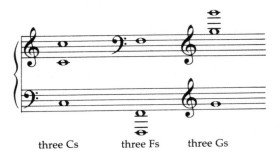

three Cs   three Fs   three Gs

Accidentals

A note which is to be raised by a semitone has a sharp sign placed in front of it.

C   C sharp

A note which is to be lowered by a semitone has a flat sign placed in front of it.

B   B flat

A note which has been raised or lowered by a semitone is returned to its natural pitch by the addition of a natural sign in front of it.

A   A flat   A natural
            again

Signs which modify the pitch of a note are called accidentals.

2   Rhythm and its notation

Stems, tails and dots

One of the great merits of staff notation is that the length and pitch of a note can be shown with one sign. This is done by using open (white) or filled (black) notes with a variety of stems, tails and dots. (The stem is the straight line.)

Notes of any length can be written at any pitch. Unless there are reasons otherwise, notes lying above the middle line have their stems down, those below have them up.

Notes on the middle line may be written either way, but look best if they conform with the surrounding notes.

The most frequent exception to this practice occurs when a number of notes are joined together with a beam.

Here the majority of the notes lie above the middle line, so the first and last note have downward stems.

The other common exception is where parts for two players or voices are written on one stave as here.

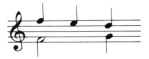

ote lengths   The two longest notes have no stems. The first of these is little used. It is a breve.   ‖○‖

Hundreds of years ago this note was one of the shortest; hence its name, meaning 'brief'.

Nowadays we count the semibreve as our whole note. All other notes are related to this.

semibreve	𝅝	whole note	1
minim	𝅗𝅥	half note	$\frac{1}{2}$
crotchet	𝅘𝅥	quarter note	$\frac{1}{4}$
quaver	𝅘𝅥𝅮	eighth note	$\frac{1}{8}$
semiquaver	𝅘𝅥𝅯	sixteenth note	$\frac{1}{16}$
demisemiquaver	𝅘𝅥𝅰	thirty-second note	$\frac{1}{32}$

Their relationship is fixed.
In other words,
one semibreve lasts as long as two minims 𝅝 = 𝅗𝅥 𝅗𝅥

one minim lasts as long as two crotchets and so on. 𝅗𝅥 = ♩ ♩

Beats

The relationship between one minim and two crotchets can be seen on paper, but what we hear in music is a beat. Any note of any value may be chosen as a beat, although the most common one-beat note is a crotchet.

Beats are grouped   in twos in duple time
in threes in triple time
in fours in quadruple time
or in fives, sixes, sevens or more.

Bars

A group of beats is called a bar and the first beat is usually stressed. A bar is marked out with bar-lines placed before each stressed note. The end of a piece is shown with a double bar-line.

Some beats might be divided into shorter notes

and sometimes a sound might last two or more beats.

Dotted notes

As there is no individual sign for a sound which lasts three-quarters of a whole note, sounds which last three crotchets are shown with a dotted minim. 𝅗𝅥.

The dot is equal to half the value of the note: $\frac{1}{2} + \frac{1}{4} = \frac{3}{4}$ of a whole note. Any note may be lengthened in the same way.

dotted crotchet ♩.

dotted quaver ♪.

ied notes

Sometimes a sound lasts longer than a bar. Two or more notes are then tied across a bar, as in this example in triple time,

where the first sound lasts eight crotchet beats.

Ties are also used for sounds which last five beats, or sub-beats, as there is no individual sign to represent this duration.

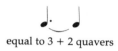

equal to 3 + 2 quavers

imple time ignatures

The number of beats in a bar is shown with a time signature. If the value of a beat was always a crotchet we would only need one figure. But as the beat can be a minim or a quaver (or in theory any other note), two figures, shown like a fraction, are required.

The upper figure gives the number of beats, the lower figure the value of the beat like this:

2 two	3 three	5 five
4 crotchets	2 minims	8 quavers
or quarter notes	or half notes	or eighth notes
in a bar	in a bar	in a bar
or their equivalent	or their equivalent	or their equivalent

The sign for four crotchet beats in a bar, $\frac{4}{4}$, is sometimes represented with a **C** . Although this is said to stand for Common time, the sign is in fact derived from the half circle that indicated medieval imperfect time, a circle having been used for the perfect triple time. Similarly, $\frac{2}{2}$ is sometimes represented with **¢** .

In simple time, the beat divides naturally into two or four equal notes.

additive me ignatures

Music in $\frac{5}{8}$ time is often fast. In practice, in place of five beats in a bar there are really just two unequal beats

like this **5/8** ♩ ♩. ♪ ♪ ⋮ ♪ ♪ ♪   or this ♩. ♩ ♪ ♪ ♪ ⋮ ♪ ♪

where one beat equals two quavers and the other three. As there is no individual note for a sound equal to three quavers, it is not possible to write a single top figure to represent it.

$$\frac{7}{8} \; \text{♩} \quad \text{♩.} \quad \text{♩} \qquad \text{or} \qquad \frac{8}{8} \; \text{♩.} \quad \text{♩.} \quad \text{♩}$$

may similarly have unequal beats.

Compound time signatures

Much more common than additive times like $\frac{5}{8}$ and $\frac{7}{8}$ are compound times, in which each beat is dotted and divides into three shorter notes. Of these, the most frequently heard is $\frac{6}{8}$ time. In this there are two dotted crotchets or their equivalent in a bar.

$$\frac{6}{8} \; \text{♩.} \quad \text{♩.}$$

Each dotted crotchet equals three quavers. It is not possible to write a single lower figure in the time signature to represent a dotted note, so the number of shorter notes into which each beat divides is given. Other examples of compound times are as follows:

6 six	or	two	or	their	(compound
4 crotchets		dotted minims		equivalent	duple time)
12 twelve	or	four	or	their	(compound
8 quavers		dotted crotchets		equivalent	quadruple time)
9 nine	or	three	or	their	(compound
16 semiquavers		dotted quavers		equivalent	triple time)

In compound times, divide the top figure by three to find the number of beats. Each beat will be dotted and equal in value to three of the notes indicated by the lower figure.

Note that in compound time a two-beat note is dotted, for just as in simple time two crotchets equal one minim, so in compound time two dotted crotchets equal one dotted minim.

$$\text{♩.} \; + \; \text{♩.} \; = \; \text{♩.}$$

In both compound and additive times, the dotted beat divides naturally into three equal notes, but also very characteristically into long and short notes of the value of $\frac{2}{3}$ and $\frac{1}{3}$; ♩. may divide into ♩ ♪ for instance.

Grouping notes

When a beat is divided, notes with tails, like quavers and semiquavers, are grouped together, so that in simple time

and in compound time

and **Exceptions to grouping in beats**

The only exceptions to grouping in beats like this are as follows:

a. In $\frac{4}{4}$ time, four quavers in either half of the bar may be grouped together.

but must never be grouped across the middle of the bar (on beats two and three), which must always be clearly seen.

b. In $\frac{3}{4}$ time, six quavers may be grouped together to form a whole bar,

and similarly, six semiquavers in $\frac{3}{8}$.

c. In traditionally printed vocal music, a single note is used for each syllable or word. Only where two or more notes are slurred over a syllable, as in a melisma, are any notes grouped together.

Sleep__in   hea__ven-ly   peace.

Until this century, this practice was universal. Nowadays, singers often prefer the notes to be grouped as in instrumental music, so that they can easily pick out the beats.

Triplets

In simple time, a beat or division of a beat sometimes divides into three instead of two or four. The group of three notes is called a triplet and is shown like this:

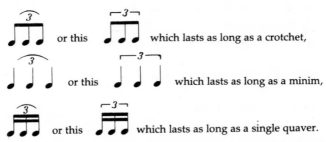

which lasts as long as a crotchet,

which lasts as long as a minim,

which lasts as long as a single quaver.

If a large number of beats divide into three, it is usually more sensible to write the music in compound time.

Duplets

Just as triplets occur in simple time, groups of two equal notes occasionally occur in compound time. These are known as duplets and are shown in two ways. Either with dotted notes like this:

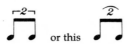

or with slurs and brackets like this:

or this

each of which in compound time would be equal to a dotted crotchet

Rests and their usage

Each note has a corresponding rest.

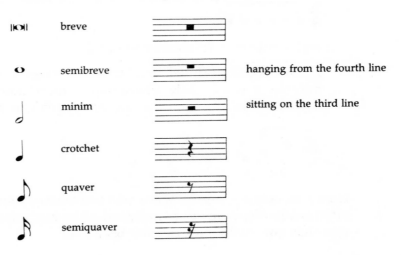

ǀ○ǀ	breve		
○	semibreve		hanging from the fourth line
♩	minim		sitting on the third line
♩	crotchet		
♪	quaver		
♬	semiquaver		

Do not use rests which are longer than one beat except as follows:

a. Where either half of a bar is silent in quadruple time.

But as with the grouping of notes, never across the middle of the bar on beats two and three.

b. Where a whole bar is silent, when a semibreve rest is used regardless of the time of the music.

The only exception to this is in the rare $\frac{4}{2}$ time, where a breve rest is used for the whole bar and a semibreve rest for the half bar.

In simple time, rests, unlike notes, are not dotted. Instead, two or more rests are used to make up the value.

In compound time, some composers and publishers show a silent beat with a dotted rest.

When making up the value of a bar with rests, complete each beat or division of a beat before moving to the next, as here:

where the quaver in the first beat is 'made up' before the remaining two silent beats are added. Or, as here:

where the semiquaver is 'made up' to a quaver, before the first beat is completed with another quaver rest and the remainder of the bar is 'made up'.

In compound time, the value of the note is completed before a rest is added in place of the dot, as here:

where the quaver is 'made up' to a crotchet before the first beat is completed with a further quaver rest. A dot might have been used in place of the final quaver rest in the second beat.

The whole process is like a transaction in a shop, where the change given (the rests) plus the cost of the purchase (the notes) must equal the amount of money tendered (the length of the bar).

3   Keys, scales and signatures

Tonic

Ninety-nine per cent of music is tonal. That is, it pulls towards a particular note which sounds final. This note was at one time called the final, but is now known as the tonic, keynote, home sound or doh.

Each tonic is like a magnet, attracting towards itself a number of sounds, which give it support. This collection of sounds forms a key. When the sounds are arranged alphabetically from the tonic, they form a scale. There are different varieties of scale, of which the two most important are the major and minor. Both have their own order of step size between pairs of notes.

Major scales

The most natural major scale is that formed on the note C. It is called the scale of C major. It stretches from one C to the next C above or below. This interval is called an octave, since it embraces eight notes. (Intervals are calculated not by the distance from one note to another but by the number of notes they embrace: thus A is one note above G but the interval G–A is a 2nd.) It uses two sizes of steps. A whole step, known as a tone, and a smaller step, known as a semitone.

Play or sing these sounds and listen to the smaller gap between E and F and B and C. Check against a keyboard. Notice that whereas the two white notes forming a tone are separated by a black note, those forming a semitone are next door to each other.

The pattern of tone–tone–semitone for the first four notes

is repeated for the second four notes.

These groups of four notes, which are separated by a tone, are called tetrachords, from the Greek words meaning four strings.

The tone–semitone pattern of steps is like a blueprint and any major scale can be constructed from it. If we take the upper tetrachord of one scale and add exactly the same arrangement of tone–tone–semitone above it, a scale with one more sharp (or one fewer flat) is formed.

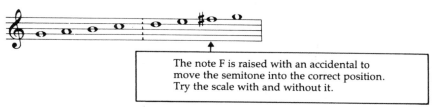

The note F is raised with an accidental to move the semitone into the correct position. Try the scale with and without it.

With the F sharp in position, the note G sounds like the tonic. The scale is in the key of G major. This procedure can be repeated over and over again to give every available scale. Each new scale will be formed on a note a 5th above the previous tonic.

Major key signatures

The accidental is moved to a position immediately after the clef and before any time signature. It becomes a key signature, and unlike the time signature it is repeated at the beginning of each line of music.

This note is F sharp; so are these.

A key signature shows that certain notes are raised or lowered by a semitone whenever they occur, even when they are in a higher or lower octave.

In tonal music, a key signature can save writing a great many accidentals. Compare this example with the previous one,

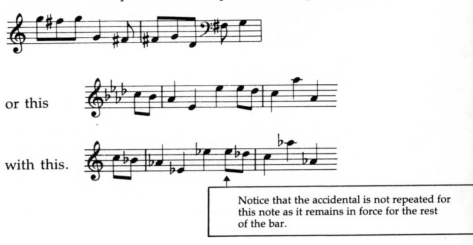

or this

with this.

Notice that the accidental is not repeated for this note as it remains in force for the rest of the bar.

A key signature has another advantage besides economising on accidentals. It allows the performer to recognize quickly the key of the piece and to tune his mind and fingers to it.

Here are the key signatures of major keys up to four sharps and flats

C major

G major

D major

A major

E major

F major

Bb major

Eb major

Ab major

Notice that the last sharp is one note below the tonic or keynote.

Notice that the last flat is a 4th above the tonic or keynote.

Modes

It seems strange that the most natural major scale starts on C instead of on A. However, in the Middle Ages a variety of scales with different tone–semitone patterns were used; these were known as modes. One was the Aeolian mode, which starts on A.

Notice the order of tones and semitones, and in particular the semitone between the second and third notes and the tone between the seventh and eighth. These make it sound very different from a major scale.

Harmonic minor scales

The Aeolian mode (along with the Dorian mode) was very popular for hundreds of years. But as with all fashions, tastes changed and a preference grew for having a semitone between the seventh and eighth notes, especially when the music was harmonised. So the seventh note was 'bent' upwards and an accidental inserted in the music.

Notice that the semitones between the second and third and the fifth and sixth notes are still as in the mode, but that another semitone has been introduced between the seventh and eighth notes.

In this form, this sequence of notes is known as a harmonic minor scale of A, or A minor harmonic. Besides the position of the three semitones, it is characterised by the gap of a tone and a half between the sixth and seventh notes.

A minor is related to C major by having the same key signature. The accidental raising the seventh note is written when required

and helps to show whether a piece is in the minor or major.

Here are the key signatures of minor keys up to four sharps and flats. The seventh-note accidental is in brackets.

A minor

E minor

D minor

B minor

G minor

F# minor

C minor

C# minor

F minor

Notice that the note leading up to F# is E# and the note leading up to C# is B#. They should never be written as F♮ and C♮ in these keys.

Notice that in C minor and F minor the accidental is a natural as it raises by a semitone a note which is flat in the key signature.

Melodic minor scales

The one-and-a-half tone gap or interval between the sixth and seventh notes of a harmonic minor scale is striking. But it is also quite difficult to sing in tune. So it is often smoothed out to make a melodic minor scale by an adjustment like this:

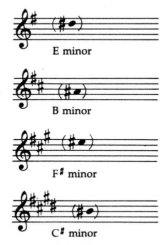

A minor melodic (ascending or upward form): sixth note raised nearer seventh note

A minor melodic (descending downward form): both seventh and sixth notes restored to the natural mode

The key signatures remain as for harmonic minor scales, all adjustments being made with accidentals.

Relative minor and major

Each major scale has a relative minor with which it shares the same key signature. The relative minor is based on the sixth note of the scale, or in other words the note next-door-but-one below the keynote. For example,

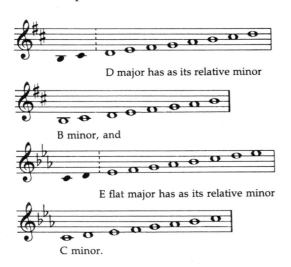

D major has as its relative minor

B minor, and

E flat major has as its relative minor

C minor.

Tonic minor

A comparison between major and minor scales built on the same tonic shows that the interval or gap between the first and third notes is one semitone less in the minor scale.

C to E
(four semitones)

C to E flat
(three semitones)

An interval of four semitones between next-door-but-one notes is called a major 3rd.

An interval of three semitones between next-door-but-one notes is called a minor 3rd.

Degrees of the scale

Each degree or note in a scale has a technical name.

The closing note of a mode was known as the final. The fifth note of many modes was called the dominant: it was frequently used in plainsong as an intoning note and therefore often dominated the music.

Nowadays the closing note or keynote in major and minor scales is called the tonic; but the fifth note is called the dominant and plays a very important part in many tonal melodies. The remaining notes of the scale are all related to these two pivotal points as can be seen from this diagram.

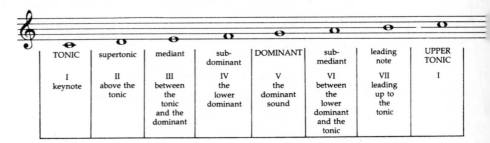

TONIC	supertonic	mediant	sub-dominant	DOMINANT	sub-mediant	leading note	UPPER TONIC
I keynote	II above the tonic	III between the tonic and the dominant	IV the lower dominant	V the dominant sound	VI between the lower dominant and the tonic	VII leading up to the tonic	I

Notice that the sub-dominant is the lower dominant, that is, the next most important note in the scale, and not just the note below the dominant.

In addition to their technical names the degrees of the scale are labelled with Roman numerals.

Chromatic scales

A complete chromatic scale has 12 different notes. Each step between one note and the next is a semitone. The technical and harmonic notation of the scale is derived from major and minor scales plus two extra notes, like this:

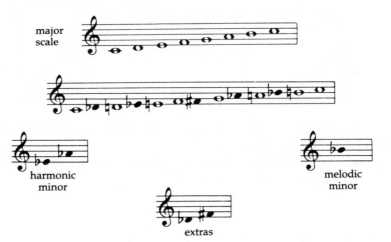

major scale

harmonic minor

melodic minor

extras

In practice, the scale is usually written in the most convenient way, avoiding accidentals where possible.

upwards using sharps

downwards using flats

A chromatic scale may be started from any note.

Pentatonic scales

As its name implies, the pentatonic scale has just five different notes. It is associated with many folk cultures (including Scottish) and dates back over two thousand years. In its most common forms it has no semitone steps.

As with the chromatic scale, a pentatonic scale can be formed on any note. Playing on the black notes of the keyboard gives a pentatonic scale.

Whole-tone scales

Again, the name whole-tone exactly defines the scale formed from six notes a tone apart. There are only two distinct versions, one starting on C, the other on C sharp or D flat.

Starting at any other point produces a scale which uses one or other of these series of notes. Again, there are no semitones and neither the pentatonic nor whole-tone scales have a strong pull towards a tonic.

4 Intervals

The distance between two sounds is called an interval. An interval is a form of measurement and always includes both the higher and lower sounds. The sounds may be played together or one after the other.

Interval size

Intervals are calculated against a scale of seven alphabetical notes, repeated as necessary. So as its name implies, an octave spans eight notes, from one letter name to the same letter name at a higher or lower pitch.

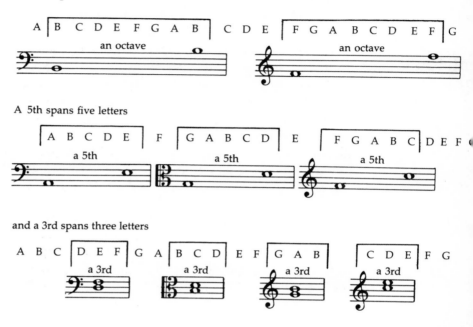

A 5th spans five letters

and a 3rd spans three letters

But as you may have noted in the paragraph on tonic minors, 3rds come in at least two forms, major 3rds (four semitones) and minor 3rds (three semitones). With shoes you can buy a size 6 in narrow, medium or broad fitting, and intervals of all sizes are qualified in a similar way.

The yardstick for measuring and qualifying intervals is the major scale.

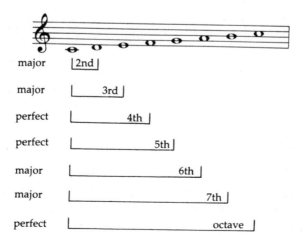

major	2nd
major	3rd
perfect	4th
perfect	5th
major	6th
major	7th
perfect	octave

In addition, when two parts play or sing the same note, the 'interval' is called a unison.

Interval quality

It is easy to see how the sizes arise. It is logical to call intervals in a major scale major intervals. It is not quite so clear why 4ths, 5ths and octaves should be called perfect. They are so called because they have a 'less flavoured' sound than other intervals, perhaps like pure water compared with lemonade or coffee! They also have a lower position in the harmonic series (see page 207) and a simpler ratio between their vibrations, e.g. the lower sound of an octave vibrates once for every two vibrations of the upper sound (1:2), whereas two notes a 5th apart vibrate in a ratio of 2:3 and two notes a 2nd apart have a ratio of 8:9.

All intervals can be expanded to make a wider interval or compressed into a narrower one. When stretched a semitone, perfect and major intervals become 'augmented'. When compressed a semitone, perfect intervals become 'diminished' and major intervals become minor. When minor intervals are compressed a further semitone they become 'diminished'.

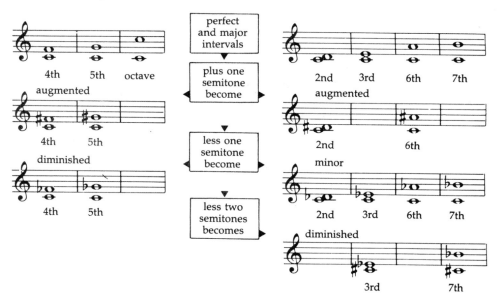

Naming intervals

When naming an interval, assume that the lower note is the tonic of a major scale. If the upper note is contained in that scale, then the interval will be perfect (4ths and 5ths) or major.

Upper note is in scale of D major, so interval is a major 6th.

If the upper note is a semitone below a scale note, the interval will be diminished (4ths and 5ths) or minor.

Upper note is semitone less than fifth degree of E major, so interval is a diminished 5th.

If the upper note is a semitone higher than the scale note, the interval will be augmented.

Upper note is semitone higher than sixth degree of E flat major, so interval is an augmented 6th.

Sometimes the upper note, especially of a 3rd or 7th, will be two semitones below the scale note, when the interval will be diminished

Upper note is two semitones lower than seventh degree of G major, so the interval is a diminished 7th.

Diminished 3rds are easily recognised as intervals which span three letter names, but which have only two semitones.

Compound intervals

An interval wider than an octave is called a compound interval. The size and quality can be calculated by imagining the lower note to be an octave higher, before proceeding as above and then adding seven (not eight) to the answer.

minor 3rd   +   7   =   minor 10th

Checking the semitones

It is sometimes helpful to check the number of semitones when naming an interval. However, before doing so, establish the size alphabetically, otherwise you may arrive at the wrong answer.

This interval has eight semitones   and spans five letter names.

This interval also has eight semitones   but spans six letter names.

The first interval is an augmented 5th, the second a minor 6th.

5   The harmonic series

When a string or column of air vibrates, it not only does so for the whole of its length, but also in parts. These partial vibrations give rise to harmonics or overtones, which are fainter in sound than the fundamental note. It is these harmonics, though, which allow us to tell the difference in sound between, for instance, an oboe and a flute.

Here is the harmonic series built on the fundamental low C:

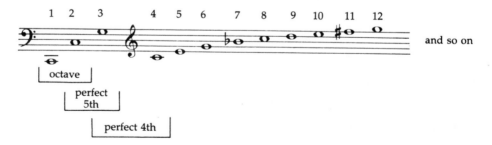

Notice the way the intervals separating the harmonics gradually grow smaller. Notice that the interval between 1 and 2 is an octave (the string vibrates in half at a ratio of 1:2), that the interval between 2 and 3 is a perfect 5th and that the interval between 3 and 4 is a perfect 4th. Then come intervals of a 3rd and, above the seventh harmonic, 2nds.

Look now at harmonics 4, 5 and 6, which, when they sound together, form a three-note chord or 'triad'.

It is this natural physical occurrence in the harmonic series which makes a common chord sound complete and satisfying. It also accounts for why the liking for chords of this pattern has dominated music for hundreds of years. In fact the harmonic series is really a giant chord of which the lowest part forms a perfectly distributed six-part major chord.

6   Chords and cadences

Although any group of two or more different notes played or sung at the same time is called a chord,

a look at the harmonic series shows why a triad formed from alternate notes of the scale is such a natural sound.

Chords in major keys

Triads or chords can be formed on each degree of the scale, although that on VII is quite different in quality from the other six.

I   II   III   IV   V   VI   VII

Except for the chord of VII, each triad spans a perfect 5th.

] perfect 5th

This interval is divided into two 3rds, one major and one minor.

Primary and secondary chords

The triads on I, IV and V have the major 3rd at the bottom and are called major triads. These are the primary chords.

] major 3rd

Those on II, III and VI have the minor 3rd in the lowest position and are minor triads. These are the secondary chords.

] minor 3rd

The triad on VII is different in sound and use and spans a diminished 5th filled in with two minor 3rds. Because of this, it is restless or unstable in effect.

] diminished 5th

Root position

The lowest sound of a triad is called the root, as it is from this note that the chord grows and gets its name. The other two sounds are called the 3rd and the 5th. Chords in root position are chords with their naming note at the bottom.

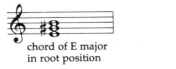
chord of E major
in root position

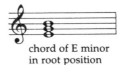
chord of E minor
in root position

Note that a chord of E minor can occur in a major key, e.g. as the chord of II in D major or the chord of III in C major.

Chords in minor keys

Although minor chords are found in major keys, they are always the secondary chords of II, III and VI.

In contrast, in a minor key without accidentals, the chords of I, IV and V are minor. However, when the leading note is raised as for a harmonic minor scale, the chord on V becomes a major chord.

In addition, the chords of II and VII are both diminished and that on III is augmented.

Because of this, chords in a minor key are just a little more difficul to use in simple progressions. Using inversions for the diminished and augmented chords helps.

Inversions

A triad or chord need not have its root as its lowest note. It can be rearranged so that the 3rd or even the 5th is at the bottom. Such arrangements are termed inversions. They are either figured to show the interval of the upper notes above the lowest note, or simply labelled with a Roman numeral followed by the letter b or c.

First-inversion chords are freely used and quite common. The chords of VII in the major and of II in the minor are rarely used other than in first inversion. Second-inversion chords have a much more restricted use and are usually linked closely with other chords.

Open position

Triads do not appear only in close position, with their notes as near as possible to one another. They may be opened up and spread more widely.

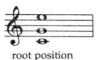
root position

first inversion

second inversion

Their labelling remains the same.

Doubling

They may also be thickened by the doubling of one or more notes, usually the root or 5th, unless the triad is minor. Vocal music naturally adopts a four-part layout for soprano, alto, tenor and bass (SATB), but both vocal and instrumental music use richer textures at times. Much keyboard music is based on a three-part texture, but may change from bar to bar, both for variety and to make playing easier.

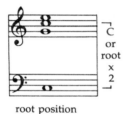
root position

first inversion

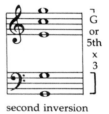
second inversion

The lowest note of the chord still determines whether the chord is in root position or in an inversion. The first example is not a second inversion as might appear from the chord in the treble clef. When using chords, always work upwards from the bass.

Dominant 7th

One much used chord has four different notes. This is the chord on the dominant with added 7th. It is called the dominant 7th.

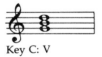
Key C: V

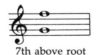
7th above root

V₇

The dominant 7th often leads to the chord of I.

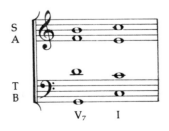

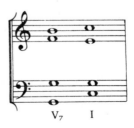

Part writing

Notice in the V₇–I examples that:

a. the bass jumps between the roots of V₇ and I
b. the upper three voices move to the closest note in the next chor
    by step or by staying still
c. the augmented 4th between soprano and alto in the dominant
    7th chord moves outwards by semitones
d. and that as a result, one chord in each example has a note
    missing, the G from the tonic chord in the first and the D from
    the dominant chord in the second.

Allowing the voices to move naturally in this way helps to avoid
weak parallel movement, which often leads to consecutive perfect
5ths and octaves. These open-sounding intervals, when they occur on
after the other, reduce the number of independent parts from four to
three or even to two. Such changes in texture when planned are ver
effective, but when they occur haphazardly here and there, they
weaken the effect of the music.

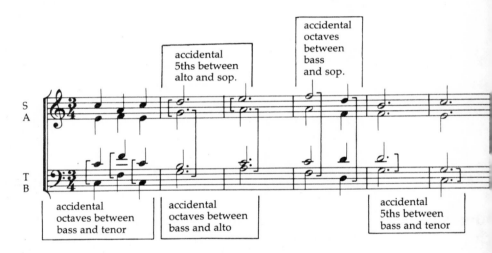

Wherever possible, avoid parallel movement by letting the bass
move in the opposite direction (in contrary motion) to the upper
parts. Where this is not possible, and the outer parts move in the
same direction (in similar motion), the bass should jump while the
top part moves by step.

Cadences

Cadences use two chords and are the simplest form of harmonic
progression. They are used, like punctuation, at the end of a musical
phrase or sentence. The progression V₇–I is one such cadence; there
are three others.

V–I
Perfect cadence

Also known as a full close. The strongest of cadences, used at the end of a piece and elsewhere as a full stop.

Bach: French Suite
no. 5 in G major

V   I

G: VI IIb ⌊V   I ⌋

V(or II)–V
Imperfect cadence

A misleading name. Also known as a half close, which is better, as it is used where the music is to continue. Open cadence might be an even better term. Used like a comma.

Beethoven: Sonata
op. 14 no. 2

IIb   V

IV   V

C: I ⌊IIb   V⌋

C: VI ⌊IV   V⌋

V–VI
Interrupted cadence

Interrupts the flow of the music. The dominant chord sounds as if it will move to the tonic, but goes off in an unexpected direction. The Americans call it a deceptive cadence. It might be thought of as being like a question or exclamation mark.

Haydn: Sonata in
D major H XVI/14

V₇   VI

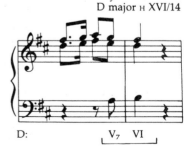

D: ⌊V₇   VI⌋

IV–I
Plagal cadence

Another cadence ending on the tonic, but much rarer than the perfect cadence. Associated with 'Amen' and with pentatonic folksongs. Seldom found in the 18th century, and then usually as a decoration of a perfect cadence.

Good King Wenceslas

IV   I

fu – – el

A: ⌊IV   I

Inversion in cadences

Sometimes one or other of the chords in a cadence will be in inversion. Where a second-inversion chord is used, it usually decorates or delays the first or second chord by coming in front of it on a stronger beat. It always has the same bass note (or its octave) as the chord it displaces.

Ic | V₇   I

Chopin: Prelude no. 22

G minor: Ic | V₇   I

When a first inversion is used in place of a root position, the cadence is less final (perhaps more like a semicolon) and it readily flows on into the next phrase.

IVc | I   Vb

*Haydn: Sonata in
F major H XVI:9*

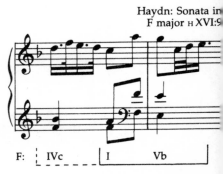

F: IVc | I   Vb

In this example, I is displaced at the beginning of the bar by IVc, before it moves to Vb in the next bar. When Ic and IVc are used in this way, they are called cadential ⁶₄s. Such chords do not change the basic pattern of the cadence. Their function is to delay and decorate. Many people consider it better to consider them as double appoggiaturas (leaning notes) or suspensions.

e use of
st
versions

First-inversion chords are more often found within the phrase than at the cadence.
They are used:

a.   to break up and add variety to a succession of root-position chords
b.   to give, where desirable, a lighter effect than that given by the stronger, firmer root-position chords
c.   to allow a smoother, more melodic bass line
d.   to overcome problems of parallel movement which arise easily with root-position chords.

Compare this, which uses root-position chords only,

with this, where Mozart uses Vb to add variety.

Mozart: Contredanse κ535

Or compare this example, where Mozart uses non-chord passing notes as well as inversions,

Mozart: German Dance к605 no.

with this solid and rather dull root-position version.

Non-chord notes

Non-chord notes are sounds used decoratively or melodically which d• not belong to the chord in use. For instance, in the second bar of the previous example, the G and Es in the tune are non-chord notes, as they do not belong to the chord of D on which the bar is based. They are sometimes known as unessential notes, since they are not any part of the essence of the chord. However, far from being unessential, as we generally use the word, they are often the 'life and soul of the party', adding movement and sometimes a spicy dissonance to the tune. There are five main types of non-chord note.

Passing notes

As in the example quoted. These move by step between different notes of the chord.

They always pass, they never jump away. Most conveniently they fill in the space between the 3rds of a triad, but they may also appear as a pair between chord notes a 4th apart.

ning notes, or
oggiaturas

These lean on the chord note on the stronger part of the beat. They may, especially in compound time, last longer than the note they lean on. They may be approached, but not left, by leap.

They were once notated by grace notes so that they could be easily spotted and their non-chord role recognised.

Where an appoggiatura is approached by step it is sometimes called an accented passing note.

Some appoggiaturas lean upwards! If they do, they can be raised a semitone, to make them more like leading notes.

uspensions

These are appoggiaturas which are 'prepared' on the previous weaker beat as part of another chord. At one time, all dissonant notes were similarly prepared. They get their name from the fact that the previous sound is suspended over the new chord (of which they are not the essence). The preparation and suspension may be tied, but do not have to be (as is sometimes thought).

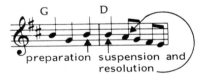

Anticipations

These are short notes which sound just before they are expected. They are usually found at a cadence in front of the last chord of the phrase or piece. They might be a direct anticipation of the next note of the melody, or an indirect anticipation, of another note of the accompanying chord which follows. They are often linked to a dotted rhythm. Unlike preparations for suspensions, anticipations do not have to belong to the chord with which they sound.

direct anticipation

indirect anticipation

Neighbouring or
auxilliary notes

These lie between the same chord notes. They may be a step above or below them. Like passing and leaning notes, they may be chromatically altered.

Here is part of the melody of a trio from Mozart's German Dance к600 no.6, with a summary of the non-chord (unessential) notes introduced.

bars	beats	
1–4		chord notes from the chord of D
5	1	chromatic leaning note rising a semitone
	2	leaning note
	3	preparation on weak beat for next bar's suspension
6	1–2	suspension (E) with detour
	3	resolution on note D, which also prepares next suspension
7	1	suspension resolving on to C sharp on next quaver
	2	leaning note
	3	chord notes of V_7 chord
9	2	chromatically altered neighbouring note

Double leaning notes and suspensions

Where leaning notes occur in two parts at the same time, they may appear to make a second-inversion chord.

IVc or leaning notes?

Where this double decoration is prepared on the previous weak beat, it becomes a double suspension, but still produces a $^6_4$ chord on the strong beat.

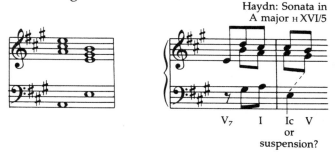

Haydn: Sonata in
A major H XVI/5

V₇   I   Ic V
or
suspension?

The effect is the same, the explanation optional.

Pedal points

A pedal point is a held or repeated note which does not always fit in with the harmony. In this sense it has some of the quality of an unessential or non-chord note and like them is not quitted except when it is part of the harmony. A pedal point is usually in the bass but may be higher, in which case it is called an inverted pedal point.

Pedal points and drones are really the same. Many folk cultures use drones as an accompaniment and sometimes composers will use pedal points when they wish to produce a rustic effect. However, pedal points have wider uses and can give rise to exciting clashes as first one chord and then another collides with the pedal point.

As with drones, pedal points are usually based on the tonic or dominant or on both.

Mendelssohn: *Volkslied* op. 53

A favourite device of Mendelssohn and Bach is to have a long tonic pedal at the end of a movement, where the music is summed up. This is known as a peroration over a tonic pedal.

7   Modulation

When a tune or piece of music moves from one key to another it is said to modulate. Many fine and well-known tunes do not modulate at all, but in longer pieces, modulation becomes part of the structure, adding direction, strength and variety. A sense of direction is felt as the music moves towards new tonal centres and then back to the original tonic. Strength comes from the opposing force of different keys, pulling and pushing against each other. Variety arises from the relative pitch of the different keys, their sharpness or flatness and their major or minor mode.

Music may modulate gradually, or jump from one key to another with little warning. Short pieces and melodies may not stay in the new key for more than a brief cadence. Most modulation is to closely related keys; that is, to keys with one flat or sharp more or fewer than the tonic. Pieces often modulate to the dominant and relative minor.

Spotting a change of key in a melody

When trying to spot a modulation, look out and listen for the perfect cadence in the new key. When the music is harmonised, there is plenty to help you, but when the melody is alone, only the tip of the cadence (as with an iceberg) may be showing.

Here are the tell-tale tips to look and listen for at any perfect cadence in a tune. They are set out diagramatically in scale degrees with examples in the tonic and three related keys.

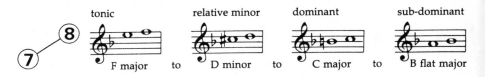

This is the easiest kind of tip to spot, because the leading note in the new key (except with the sub-dominant) will have an accidental.

While shepherds watched their flock

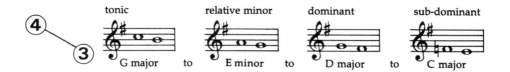

This is harder as no accidental (except with the sub-dominant) will guide you in closely related keys. It implies the sound of the 7th of the dominant 7th falling to the 3rd of the new tonic chord.

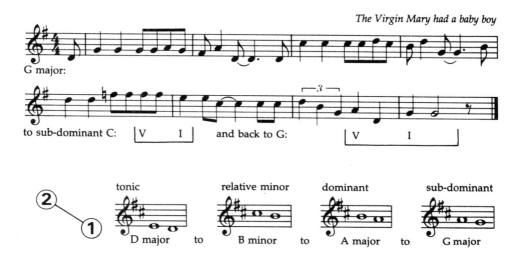

Again no accidental in the melody, but a feeling of moving down firmly to rest on the new tonic.

In each of the above examples, the first note or the cadence would be harmonised with the dominant or dominant 7th chord in the new key.

Summary of major tune modulation

Modulation to the *dominant* may take place at the end of the first phrase or in the middle. Look out for an extra sharp or one flat fewer on the way.

Modulation to the *relative minor* may take place before or after this. Look out for the raised dominant, i.e. G sharp in C major or B sharp in E major.

Modulation to the *sub-dominant* sometimes comes in the first bar or two, but is most likely towards the end. Look out for the 7th of the home key being flattened.

Minor tune modulation

Minor tunes modulate to their relative major or, less frequently, to the dominant or sub-dominant minor. For instance:

C minor to E flat major (very common)
C minor to G minor   (less common)
C minor to F minor   (less common)

Harmonised modulation

When harmonies are present, it is usually easier to recognize modulations. Listen and look for the perfect cadence in the new key. It is usually approached through the chord of II, IV or VI in the new key, which may have these chords in common with the old key. The dominant 7th chord of the new key will always include at least one accidental.

The well-known Christmas hymn *It came upon a midnight clear* illustrates a number of cadences and modulations.

Sullivan: *It came upon a midnight clear*

F major: imperfect I V   plagal IV I

imperfect I V   perfect Ic V₇ I   no modulation to here

modulation to relative minor   modulation to dominant
to D minor: II₇ V₇ I   to C major: Ic V₇ I

modulation to relative minor of sub-dominant and back to F major
G minor: V₇ I   F major: Ic V₇ I

Index